THE
LAST MYTH

ALSO BY MATHEW BARRETT GROSS

The Glen Canyon Reader (as editor, 2003)

THE
LAST MYTH

WHAT THE RISE OF
APOCALYPTIC THINKING
TELLS US ABOUT AMERICA

MATHEW BARRETT GROSS
MEL GILLES

 Prometheus Books

59 John Glenn Drive
Amherst, New York 14228–2119

Published 2012 by Prometheus Books

Cover image © 2012 Media Bakery
Cover design by Grace M. Conti-Zilsberger

Inquiries should be addressed to
Prometheus Books
59 John Glenn Drive
Amherst, New York 14228–2119
VOICE: 716–691–0133
FAX: 716–691–0137
WWW.PROMETHEUSBOOKS.COM

16 15 14 13 12   5 4 3 2 1

Library of Congress Cataloging-in-Publication Data

Gross, Mathew Barrett, 1972–
    The last myth : what the rise of apocalyptic thinking tells us about America / by Mathew Barrett Gross and Mel Gilles.
        p. cm.
    Includes bibliographical references and index.
    ISBN 978–1–61614–573–6 (pbk. : alk. paper)
    ISBN 978–1–61614–574–3 (ebook)
    1. End of the world. 2. Attitude (Psychology)—United States. 3. Public opinion—United States. 4. United States—Forecasting. I. Gilles, Mel, 1973– II. Title.

BL503.G76 2012
306.4—dc23

2011045846

Printed in the United States of America on acid-free paper

For each other

"The truly apocalyptic view of the world is that things do not repeat themselves. It isn't absurd e.g., to believe that the age of science and technology is the beginning of the end for humanity; that the idea of great progress is a delusion, along with the idea that the truth will ultimately be known; that there is nothing good or desirable about scientific knowledge and that mankind, in seeking it, is falling into a trap. It is by no means obvious that this is not how things are."

—Ludwig Wittgenstein, *Culture and Value* (1947)

". . . and you said, *This isn't America* into the truck's dark cab and turned the radio loud."

—Kevin Prufer, "We Wanted to Find America" (2008)

CONTENTS

INTRODUCTION

THE END OF
THE WORLD?

In America, everyone believes in the apocalypse. The only question is whether Jesus or global warming will get here first.

As the twenty-first century enters its tween years, we are faced with a seemingly inexhaustible supply of scenarios for how the world might end. Evangelical Christians find signs of the end times in the worsening news from the Middle East. Economists, wounded investors, and the legions of unemployed continue to ponder whether a nation that once fueled its growth on easy credit and a speculative housing boom will ever recover from the economic collapse that arrived when the free money dried up and the mortgage came due. Political activists increasingly question whether the democracy that is our birthright will survive an age of corporate-controlled media and touch-screen voting machines. During the first decade of this century, Democrats doubted whether the nation could survive the shredding of the Constitution by President George W. Bush; nowadays, Republicans and Tea Partiers insist the nation won't survive the shredding of free-market principles by President Barack Obama. Outside the political realm, scientists speculate about when and how—not if—our unabated addiction to fossil fuels will bring about widespread climate change. Biologists tell us that whole ecological systems are collapsing, that we are literally watching the world disappear before our eyes, that we are living through the greatest mass-extinction event since the dinosaurs. And every day, for ordinary Americans, the ever-worsening news flashes across our television and computer screens, the images suffusing our collective consciousness. From gushing oil wells in the Gulf of Mexico to nuclear disaster in Japan, from the war on terror to the skyrocketing national debt, everywhere we look there's a horseman—dressed as a warrior, ecologist, economist, or preacher—to herald that the end is near.

Indeed, no matter which scenario du jour is capturing our imagination, one single thought unites all Americans in these fiercely partisan times: the belief that the American way of life is heading rapidly toward the edge of a cliff—if we haven't already gone over it.

This sense that a final reckoning moment is imminent—a collapse, as the secularists would call it, or the Rapture, as evangelicals would dream it—has been growing in power and influence since the dawn of the nuclear age. Since the year 2000, however, that growth has accelerated. A 2002 poll commissioned by *Time* magazine found that 59 percent of Americans believe that the events foretold in the book of Revelation will come true; an expectation of an apocalypse is not an anomaly in American culture but a view held by the majority.[1] Tim LaHaye and Jerry Jenkins's Left Behind series—which tells the story of the travails of those who are left on earth after the Rapture—sold more than sixty-three million copies in the first decade of the new millennium.[2] The Christian vision of the end times has become so commonplace that in March of 2006, President George W. Bush was asked during a nationally televised press conference: "Do you believe . . . that the war in Iraq and the rise of terrorism are signs of the apocalypse?"[3]

Such questions about (and obsessions with) the end of the world are not confined to the Christian Right, of course. Former vice president Al Gore has parlayed his warnings of a catastrophic future into a bestselling book, an Academy Award–winning documentary, and a Nobel Peace Prize. The historian Jared Diamond dominated the *New York Times* nonfiction bestseller list through much of the 2000s by capturing the decade's zeitgeist, dressing it in footnotes, and selling it back to a liberal middle class increasingly nervous about its ecological future.[4] For the first time in its history, the Pulitzer Prize for Fiction went not to an epic family saga or a suburban melodrama but to a postapocalyptic sci-fi potboiler— Cormac McCarthy's 2006 *The Road*. Meanwhile, books examining the coming crisis of peak oil, expounding on the meaning of the year 2012, or debating whether hyperinflation or a deflationary collapse will deliver the coup de grâce to the Great Recession have been scooped up by secular readers who seem certain that disaster—in one form or another—lies just around the bend.

Or does it? In those rare moments when we take a step back to survey the dour hysteria and apocalyptic jeremiads that today define our nation, we find ourselves waving a hand in a dismissive gesture and telling ourselves, with an embarrassed laugh, that people have always thought this way—as though our own dim view of the future might somehow be disqualified if we could just prove its historical consistency. "People have always believed in the end of the world," we tell ourselves, in hopeful self-deprecation. "Haven't they?"

With that question in mind, journalists set out every few months, with an almost metronomic consistency, to get the story of Chicken Little in America. Writing for *Harper's* or the *Atlantic* or *Time*, they chronicle a subculture—Christian evangelicals, survivalists, peak-oil theorists—in an attempt to understand why people are so predisposed to believe the sky is falling. The apocalypse, they conclude, has always been the hobgoblin of the conspiratorial mind, a subject best treated with a dismissive shake of the head. Some people are just plain *weird*.

Yet to dismiss our contemporary apocalyptic beliefs with an imagined historical relativism ("People have always thought this way.") or a strained journalistic conceit ("Only other people think this way.") is to miss the larger story. We have reached a sort of mocking détente in America—with the Left scoffing at the Rapture, and the Right rejecting the science behind global warming—at the expense of understanding the common lens through which most Americans are now looking at the world. The apocalyptic ideal has vaulted from religious esoterica to pop culture headline; yesterday's disheveled whackos are today's American middle class. The widespread belief in *some* kind of apocalypse is the defining cultural phenomenon of our time, and its popularity has something profound to tell us about the American mind-set—and the past, present, and future of America—as we enter the second decade of the twenty-first century.

*   *   *

For a subject matter that has leapt from the edges of society to the forefront of a presidential press conference, the apocalypse has received surprisingly little serious scrutiny. Scientists nervously add a string of caveats when their research suggests it. Academic studies of the apocalypse are relegated to esoteric texts on literary theory. When the apocalypse shows up in Hollywood films and novels, it is usually in a strikingly puerile manner—as a backdrop for picaresque adventure stories. And politicians understandably avoid it altogether. When George W. Bush was asked whether he believed that the war in Iraq and the rise of terrorism were signs of the apocalypse, his response was both unbelievable and telling. Despite being the president of a nation awash in apocalyptic beliefs and the leader of a Republican Party that had crafted political dominance by catering to fundamentalist Christians, he claimed that the question was the "first I've heard of that" and then dismissed the concept by declaring, "I'm a practical man."[5]

Such dismissals leave a great number of people feeling that their own widely held apocalyptic visions (whether religious, scientific, economic, or environmental) are marginal at best and crazy at worst. Yet Americans increasingly have turned to apocalyptic metaphors to explain and understand a world and nation that look radically different from just a decade ago. In the absence of any other explanatory narrative—which our media, failing spectacularly at placing the news it reports into a larger context, rarely offers—the apocalypse serves as a way of coping with "unprecedented" events, offering the promise that the chaos of our times will eventually prove to have some kind of redemptive meaning.

The word *apocalypse* comes to us from the Greek, and it means literally "the lifting of the veil"—a time when all things are revealed. In our culture, the word is used as shorthand for the more accurate phrase *apokalupsis eschaton*—"the revelation of knowledge at the end of time." By the narrowest and most academic definition, a true apocalypse is a literary genre of Jewish or Christian texts written between the second century BCE and the second century CE, like the book of Daniel or the book of Revelation.

Yet these days, the apocalypse is no longer just a book in the Bible; it is a pattern of thought that assumes that the end of our way of life (if not physically the end of the world itself) is imminent. Whether one longs for or fears a religious or secular apocalypse, this "end of the world" will come in a moment, a moment that will present the final showdown between opposing forces or viewpoints—the definitive end to the ongoing argument between Christians and non-Christians, or between crunchy environmentalists and SUV-driving consumers. The consolation of looking forward to that moment—whatever it may be—comes from its validation of the believer's worldview. The Rapture rewards the devout Christian; global warming, in a less victorious way, validates the environmentalist's warnings about our relationship to nature. Regardless of the scenario, in the modern version of apocalypse, the end of the world isn't random—it proves a point, once and for all.

Identifying the apocalypse as an explanatory narrative for the accelerating changes facing us in the twenty-first century helps us understand the apocalypse's predominance in our culture and its application by ordinary people to a range of issues, from the collapse of the housing bubble to the threat of epidemics. It also explains why so many people, dissatisfied by the current state of our nation and culture, turn to the apocalypse and its signs as both a vindication and a consolation.

*   *   *

The apocalypse is a story that all of us *think* we know. Yet many of our assumptions about that story—that other cultures have had similar expectations of the end of the world, or that people at all times have believed in equal measure that the end is near—prove, on closer examination, to be false. These days, the apocalypse in America is as familiar as a catchy pop song, and the melody and the lyrics resonate so deeply with us that it feels like we've known the song forever. But despite their resonance, of course, the melody and the lyrics started somewhere. In the same way, apocalyptic thinking has a historical beginning; a belief in the end of the world is neither a universal trait nor a biological imperative.[6] People haven't always hummed this tune, though for the past two thousand years in Western culture, it's been a recurring hit—particularly in times of crisis.

Apocalyptic expectation has surged into the mainstream during the great upheavals in Western history and thought—at those moments when people intrinsically felt that their place in history was unsustainable. It was there when the Israelites first began to imagine history not as a meaningless place but as the place where the will of God unfolded. It was there during the Reformation, when millions in Europe turned away from the perceived corruption and venality of the Catholic Church. And it persisted in America among fundamentalist Christians who grew increasingly alarmed by the rapid industrialization and secularization of society throughout much of the nineteenth century.

Given the resurgence of apocalyptic expectation in America in the past dozen years, the question naturally arises: Are we, too, at such a moment of upheaval? It is clear that we are living in one of the greater transitional times in the history of our republic. The American middle class is disappearing under the weight of household debt, even as the wealthiest Americans strengthen their grip on a greater and greater share of national assets; "the era of easy oil is over," is no longer the murmur of conspiracy nuts but the tagline of a national advertising campaign by one of our nation's largest oil companies; and the American military is mired in an already decade-long war in Afghanistan and seemingly incessant military interventions around the world. Meanwhile, the American political system appears incapable of addressing any of the mounting issues before us. The American way of life may not be negotiable, as former vice president Dick Cheney famously said at the beginning of this new century, but to an ever-increasing majority of our population, it doesn't seem quite sustainable either.[7]

The instability of our world and our place within it forces us to ask some questions about our addiction to apocalyptic thinking. As Americans, are we predisposed to adopt an apocalyptic worldview in times of crisis, regardless of our religious upbringing? Why is the apocalypse surging now? Is thinking apocalyptically a help or a hindrance? If the latter, how might we move beyond the apocalypse as a means of understanding the world? And are any of the current crises we face truly apocalyptic?

As real and threatening crises mount on the horizon of the twenty-first century, understanding how our daydreams of doomsday are coming between us and our ability to confront global challenges has never been more urgent. But conflating our expectation of the apocalypse with the issues before us is an error: the apocalypse is a belief; the challenges facing us are real. To intertwine the two in either direction is dangerous: to discount real crises because they resemble myth in scale is foolishness; to disregard how apocalyptic belief impinges our ability to address those problems is equally imprudent. This book is not about predicting the end of the world, or about how one might prepare for calamity, or about debating when the apocalyptic moment will arrive. Rather, this book is an exploration of our transformative time and place and of what it means to live in a culture that is overwhelmingly consumed by the belief that the end—however we imagine it—is nearly here.

CHAPTER 1

THE APOCALYPTIC DECADE

Few of us can clearly make out the form of history until it is well behind us. The current events that preoccupy us, which we imbue with so much meaning in our daily lives, are often found years later to be of little consequence. The past has another pattern, as T. S. Elliot wrote[1]—and while we look elsewhere or speak of other things, history manifests itself in the wings of the stage. The subplots become the main narrative, and what we perceived as the central crisis of our lives is often later revealed to be a minor and slightly flawed scene, the terrible acting of which is quickly forgotten.

Only in retrospect do the more lasting images and themes of an era reveal themselves. We think of flappers and fur coats and a youthful decadence when we think of the Roaring Twenties. Goose-stepping newsreel fascists in Europe carry the banners emblazoned with our memory of the thirties, segueing into the ticker-tape victory parades of the forties. A cloistered conformity has defined the fifties; hippies, the sixties; self-indulgence, the seventies; and greed, the eighties. Yet while history is happening—while the present is slipping into that inevitable and simplifying parody that soon enough becomes the past—few of us can correctly identify what will later be seen as the dominant cultural icon

of our era. A housewife in Peoria in 1967 had little comprehension
that her decade would be remembered not for any of the things
that consumed her daily life but for the kids who had just driven
past her house in a VW® Bus, leaving a scent of grass and patchouli
in their wake as they turned down the next block.

That we are blinded to history by our own proximity to current
events helps us understand why we still have not settled on a
common name for the decade now receding behind us. "The
Aughts" never caught on, in part because "aught" as a reference to
"zero" remains largely alien to the American vernacular. "The
Zeros" is too dreary—too steeped in self-abnegation and too rem-
iniscent of what became of our 401(k)s as the decade came to a
close—for even the most maudlin among us to choose it. Some
have suggested "The Terror Decade" for obvious reasons, but such
a designation fails to encompass the full spectrum of events that
influenced the receding decade's mood. How others will look back
on this time is beyond our knowing or influence, of course, but
future historians would do well to ascribe to our time a name that
encapsulates not just the events of the past decade but the way in
which we as Americans have come to view the world and our place
within it. Such a name might be the Apocalyptic Decade or, perhaps, the Apocalyptic Era—for it is not over yet.

It was during the last decade, after all, that the belief in the end
of the world leapt from the cultish into the mainstream of American society. Ours is an era bookended by the widespread belief in
the impending collapse of society: at one end we had Y2K, the
largest and most expensive mass preparation for a secular apocalypse in the history of the world; at the other end we have the
growing expectation and belief that December 21, 2012—the supposed end date of the ancient Mayan Long Count calendar—will

herald either a radically transformative or utterly cataclysmic global event. Between these two bookends are pages upon pages of apocalyptic anxiety, a decade-plus-long collection that tells the tale of an America that has grown very afraid of the future.

Ours is a country whose optimism and can-do spirit won two world wars and put a man on the moon during the twentieth century; a nation that has given humankind, in the space of less than a hundred years, the dream of flight, the wonder of electricity, and the power of the Internet. And yet today, Americans of all beliefs and backgrounds are turning increasingly to apocalyptic scenarios to explain and understand a world and nation that look radically different from just a decade ago. This turn toward the apocalyptic is understandable. After all, the headlines of our age read like a horrific disaster novel, with the first chapter titled 9/11; the second chapter, Hurricane Katrina; the third chapter, the Great Recession; and on and on. Nearly every news story—from those dealing with terrorism to climate change to a global economy coming apart at the seams—appears to point to an impending end of the way of life that we have known.

The news looks bad, to be sure. Yet Americans have faced bad news and great challenges before, while largely managing to keep apocalyptic despair off the airwaves and out of presidential press conferences. How have we come to interpret nearly every event through the prism of the apocalypse?

THE END OF HISTORY

To answer that question, it helps to first remind ourselves that we haven't always thought as apocalyptically about world events as we do today. American history is filled with extended periods when the nation looked at the challenges it faced not with despair but with optimism; times when we felt with certainty that the country was not only on the right track but was traveling with great speed toward what would surely be a glorious destination. Such periods are not relegated solely to the distant past. Indeed, though we often forget it, we experienced an extended period of such optimism a little more than twenty years ago, when the Cold War came to an end.

As the Soviet Union collapsed and our four-decades-long fear of nuclear annihilation receded, a heavy burden was removed from our shoulders, and a new sense of levity arose around us. On the pop charts, British rock band Jesus Jones sang about the joy of sitting before the television set as history appeared to come to an end.[2] This was, as another song went, the end of the world as we'd known it—and we felt fine. The long struggle between Western democracy and communism hadn't ended in a nuclear conflagration but instead with the opening of a McDonald's in Moscow. The music at Bill Clinton's inaugural gala in 1993 perfectly (if somewhat embarrassingly) captured the mood of the adolescent decade: yesterday was gone, indeed.

The sense of historical emancipation felt during the early 1990s is best exemplified by American philosopher and political economist Francis Fukuyama's influential essay "The End of History?"[3] Fukuyama borrowed his title from Karl Marx (who had, in turn, borrowed it from Hegel) to argue that the end of the Cold War signaled the triumphant end to human progress. "What we may be witnessing," Fukuyama wrote of the current events swirling around him, as the Berlin Wall fell and Eastern Europe broke free of Soviet influence, "is not just the end of the Cold War or the passing of a particular period of post-war history, but *the end of history*."[4] Like Hegel and Marx before him, Fukuyama viewed history as a struggle between competing ideologies—in Fukuyama's case, between Western liberal democracy and the authoritarianism of fascism and communism. The collapse of the Soviet Union, in Fukuyama's mind, marked "the end point of mankind's ideological evolution and the universalization of Western liberal democracy as the final form of human government."[5] With the fall of the Berlin Wall, the long struggle of history had finally come to an end: democracy and capitalism, empowered by rapid advances in technology, had won the global battle for the hearts and minds (not to mention the pocketbooks) of humanity.

The assertion that there would come a time when there would "be no further progress in the development of underlying principles and institutions," as Fukuyama put it, "because all of the really big questions will have been settled,"[6] had been long anticipated in Western philosophy and Judeo-Christian theology. Others had made similar proclamations of the arrival of a new Golden Age in the past. What was remarkable about Fukuyama's pronouncement at the start of the 1990s, however, was the readiness of America's academic, economic, and political elite to embrace the idea that a post-historical era had finally arrived. On Wall Street, Fukuyama's assertion that we had been emancipated from the trials of history soon morphed into the irrationally exuberant belief that the "new economy" of the dot-com boom marked a liberation from the fundamental laws of economics.

Meanwhile, in Washington, DC, the notion that we had reached a point where the supremacy of democratic capitalism was indisputable reverberated around the corridors of the nation's capital and echoed in the inner sanctums of both political parties. The concepts of Fukuyama's book *The End of History* rang through the philosophical justifications for the policies of free-market globalization pursued by President Bill Clinton, who argued that globalization was inevitable—"an economic force of nature"[7] that would lift people in third-world countries (or those who were still "mired in history,"[8] as Fukuyama put it) up to our own level of post-historical prosperity. At the other end of the political spectrum, Fukuyama's ideas were cribbed by the Project for the New American Century (PNAC), the neoconservative think tank whose members and leadership included Fukuyama himself, Dick Cheney, Donald Rumsfeld, Paul Wolfowitz, Lewis Libby, and William Kristol. PNAC's vision of a new Pax Americana—in which the United States would "build up material wealth at an accelerated rate"[9] through the securing of global resources and maintain its ideological preeminence through military might—would become the philosophical and strategic basis for the Bush doctrine of preemptive war following the attacks of September 11, 2001.

There were shortcomings to this new glib Golden Age of the 1990s, however. In retrospect, it relied too much on the pronouncements of financial analysts and academics, who loudly repudiated the laws of economics and the lessons of history. America was on top, they promised, and would be forevermore. Soon, we would all be able to cash in our Yahoo! stock and retire poolside to while away the days in an eternally blissful Margaritaville. If such statements now seem hyperbolic, it's worth remembering the ink that was spilled in the early 1990s by journalists and commentators who wondered what effects the end of the Cold War and the surging NASDAQ might have on our once-pioneering spirit. Fukuyama, for example, feared that the end of history would prove a "sad time" because its luxuriously soporific victors would lack a sense of meaningful struggle. What lay ahead for humankind were "centuries of boredom" in which we in the West risked being emasculated by the "satisfaction of . . . consumer demands." We would become Nietzsche's vision of the Last Man, made despicably effeminate by the absence of any real challenges. The best eternity had to offer those of us who had inherited the post-historical world, Fukuyama lamented, were the distractions of the television set and the computer screen. The Golden Age would be, regrettably, rather dull.[10]

Looking back on the post-historical rhetoric of the early 1990s arouses feelings similar to those elicited when one reflects on the naïveté of one's youth—for the decade that followed would prove neither dull nor particularly golden. Yet it's important to remember the earnestness of the delusion that we had escaped history—a delusion that spread from Washington to the NASDAQ to the Top 40 charts—for it represents the starting point in our bipolar shift in consciousness toward apocalyptic despair. Our exuberant optimism would soon boomerang back at us. From the highest hopes come the deepest disappointments.

THE BEGINNING OF THE END

All of us remember the apocalyptic anticipation that surrounded Y2K and the approach of the new millennium. But few of us draw the right lessons from it.

Concerns first emerged in the early 1990s that a design flaw in the binary method that computer systems used to store and understand dates would cause widespread computer malfunctions when the year 2000 arrived. These malfunctions, experts predicted, would have real-world impacts, with the potential to wreak havoc on the nation's computer-reliant infrastructure. A series of government and industry reports confirmed that the "Y2K bug," as it became known, was real; failure to address the problem, the experts warned, could have an unforeseeable but potentially catastrophic impact on the nation's financial, electrical, and distribution networks.

In response to the perceived crisis, the US government and US industries began investing massive amounts of capital in upgrades to their computer networks by the middle of the 1990s. Yet despite these precautions, worry over what the year 2000 might bring soon began to spread from IT departments and corporate boardrooms to mainstream media and Main Street, USA.

We all remember what happened next. Nearly every American journalist, it seemed, secretly had an inner science fiction nerd just waiting to get out—and the idea of Y2K soon sent their imaginations running wild. "At the stroke of midnight on Dec. 31, 1999," one journalist wrote in the *San Jose Mercury News* in May of 1998, "the 'Y2K' bug will strike. Some of the big computers that run corporations and governments, and some of the tiny computers that run appliances and industrial equipment, *will suddenly freeze or go crazy*."[11] The evening news teemed with breathless reports speculating on the innumerable catastrophes that could befall a world at the mercy of these insane computer chips. Banks might lose all records of your checking and savings accounts, in effect swallowing the nest eggs of millions of helpless Americans; the computerized flight controls of modern jetliners could go haywire, sending passengers plummeting to the earth; the national power grid could shut down, plunging the nation into freezing darkness in the middle of winter; computer-controlled dams could open their floodgates, releasing a biblical deluge on American cities and towns; and the launch systems of American and Russian ICBMs could activate, raining nuclear holocaust down on the world in what would surely have been the most egregious technological screwup in history. And on and on and on, an endless invocation of technological mayhem, large and small: your car refusing to start; mass starvation arising as the food distribution system comes to a halt; your toaster defiantly refusing to brown your bagel. Anything—and everything—could happen.

The American people responded to the approaching disaster as they responded to nearly every crisis that has confronted them since the end of the Second World War—by shopping. Manufacturers of portable generators couldn't keep up with consumer demand, despite massive increases in production, and sales of everything from freeze-dried food to first-aid kits skyrocketed. As the countdown to apocalypse approached, the stocked pantries of families who had prepared for disaster became a staple of local television news. While the media's coverage of those who had gone to the furthest extremes in their preparation—selling their houses in cities and suburbs and moving to a rural acreage in anticipation of a calamitous regression to preindustrial life—tended toward the bemused, a majority of Americans followed the advice of both the federal government and the American Red Cross, who urged the stockpiling of food and water as part of their "Y2K Preparedness" bulletins. By the time New Year's Eve 2000 arrived, Americans had spent millions of man-hours and more than $300 billion for what was (to date) the most widespread and expensive preparation for a potential apocalypse in history.

And then—nothing. As the shadow of the 1990s receded across the globe and the sun rose upon the new decade, reports came in from Sydney and Tokyo and Beijing that the future had arrived not with a bang, nor even a whimper, but with an overwhelming and remarkably uneventful indifference. Americans breathed a sigh of relief—or uttered a curse of chagrin as they shut down their overpriced backup generators—as each time zone entered the new millennium without even a minor catastrophe to vindicate a cupboard full of dehydrated beans.

Almost as soon as the new decade dawned, we began to look back on Y2K with suspicion. The failure of the New Year to produce any major glitches (much less any end-of-the-world disasters) convinced many Americans that our government and media had overhyped the threat of computerized mayhem. For some, Y2K came to be seen as little more than the latest example in a long series of failed apocalyptic prophesies, indistinguishable from the predictions of Nostradamus or the end-of-the-world expectations of numerous cults and sects throughout the ages. And for many others, the whole thing came to be seen as a hoax—a con game conceived by greedy computer geeks eager to cash in on a nation's technological illiteracy.

Rather than a crisis that failed to materialize or a crisis that never existed, however, Y2K was in fact a crisis successfully averted. Of course, the media hype of what might have happened was overblown—there was little chance of your toaster going crazy, after all. Yet most IT experts today view the government and corporate investment in repairing the Y2K problem as both necessary and beneficial.[12] Thus, instead of viewing Y2K as a failed prophecy, a more accurate comparison for Y2K is the global response to the discovery of the hole in the ozone layer above Antarctica in 1987. In both cases, the world came together and made the investments and changes necessary to avert disaster. Yet for many Americans, our success in averting disaster has become evidence that the disaster was overhyped or nonexistent from the start.

Dismissing Y2K as hype, hoax, or failed prophecy is to draw the wrong lessons from the seminal moment of the Apocalyptic Decade—a moment that has a great deal to tell us about the era we are now living in. Rather than an atypical moment in our recent history—an uncharacteristic indiscretion on the part of an otherwise rational nation—Y2K was an archetypical one, setting the template for how we would perceive and react to the gathering crises of the twenty-first century.

Our reaction to Y2K demonstrated the profound ability of apocalyptic thinking to adapt to the challenges of the new millennium. Confined to the religious arena for nearly two thousand years, the apocalypse had (understandably) loomed large in the secular mind with the advent of the nuclear bomb and rising Cold War fears of atomic annihilation. If the end of the Cold War had convinced some that history had come to a peaceable end and that apocalyptic anticipation would recede into the various evangelical denominations from which it had sprung, however, Y2K proved otherwise. The optimism exemplified by Fukuyama at the beginning of the 1990s had been quickly replaced by a deep distrust in the stability of the new Golden Age. It was one thing to intertwine apocalyptic fear and rhetoric with the fear of nuclear holocaust; it was another thing altogether to witness the apocalyptic archetype interject itself into concerns over a few lines of programming in our computers. If the apocalypse could find its way into binary code, then it could—and would—find its way into our interpretation of almost any challenge before us. The apocalypse, as Y2K demonstrated, had become deeply rooted in the secular American mind.

Our failure to correctly interpret what Y2K meant has had a profound influence on how we have interpreted the challenges of our new century. As the events and trends of our own age have become ever more apocalyptic and frightening—from terrorism to global warming to the collapse of the housing bubble to the threat of energy depletion—we've looked back on the thwarted apocalyptic expectation of Y2K with a sense of confusion. Should the gathering problems before us be taken seriously or not? For some, the lack of drama or disaster that accompanied Y2K justified placing most discussions of Armageddon on the yonder side of the grassy knoll, in tinfoil-hat territory. This line of thinking has proven disastrous to efforts to address numerous pressing issues—global warming being chief among them. Yet for many others, Y2K turned obsessing about the apocalypse into a national pastime; by 2001, the expectation that a major event could lead to the rapid unraveling of modern society had moved firmly from the realm of the conspiracy into the suburban American living room, where it has stayed ever since.

Indeed, Y2K established the tone for the decade to follow. The end was right around the corner, and everyone should get ready for it; but you couldn't take it too seriously, or prepare too much, because it might not happen. In any case, the apocalyptic rhetoric that surrounded us was probably just a smoke screen so that Al Gore or Halliburton could make a buck. The coming decade's events would only reinforce this new mainstream predilection for confused apocalyptic thinking. And our reaction to those events would highlight the truly enduring lesson of Y2K, which is this: thinking apocalyptically has undermined our ability to gauge the magnitude of the global challenges now rushing toward us.

THE PROPHETIC SPEEDOMETER OF END-TIME ACTIVITY

For those who thought the apocalypse could be laid to rest with the uneventful passing of Y2K, the events of the coming decade would soon prove otherwise. Fewer than twenty-one months after Y2K, the language of apocalypse would be deployed by President Bush to provide the context and explanation for the attacks of 9/11, pushing the apocalyptic even further into the center of public debate—and sending the Rapture Index soaring.

Todd Strandberg, a born-again Christian and staff sergeant in the US Air Force, founded the Rapture Index in the mid-1980s. Like many evangelical Christians, Strandberg scoured the daily news for signs that the Tribulation (the tumultuous days prophesied in the Bible that would likely precede the return of Christ) was near.[13] As Strandberg (and millions of others) believed, nearly any event could serve as proof that the Tribulation was coming, from border skirmishes in the Middle East to disagreements within the Catholic Church to earthquakes in Nevada. Yet Strandberg soon became frustrated by the wild and wildly varied interpretations that many evangelical Christians gave to the daily news. Prophetic Christians, as Strandberg recounts, couldn't even agree on whether earthquakes—a sure sign that the end was near—were increasing or decreasing in frequency. "If people can't even count something as simple as tectonic movements of the earth," Strandberg wondered, "what yardstick would they possibly use to measure something like apostasy?"[14]

Inspired by the Dow Jones Industrial Average stock market index, Strandberg assembled a list of forty-five indicators that the Tribulation was close at hand—from the appearance of false Christs and financial unrest, to the rise of liberalism and the decay of moral standards, to the increase of unusual weather activity—and organized each of these indicators into a category, which was awarded a numeric value. Adding the numbers together produced a moving average—the standardized yardstick for which Strandberg had longed so as to measure the progression of biblical prophecy.

To clarify that the index wasn't measuring the proximity of the Rapture itself—the timing of the Rapture was unknowable, God's great surprise, as likely to arrive in calm or chaos—Strandberg dubbed the index "the prophetic speedometer of end-time activity." "The higher the number, the faster we're moving towards the occurrence of a pre-tribulation rapture," Strandberg explained.[15]

As the Rapture Index soared on 9/11, President Bush, a self-attested born-again Christian, turned immediately to the language of apocalypse to explain the attacks. In his televised address to the nation from the Oval Office on the evening of September 11, Bush described America's new battle against Islamic extremism as a battle between good and evil. To be clear, Bush was not the first president to describe America's enemies as evil, nor was he the first to use quasi-religious language to rally a nation to a larger struggle. Nor, for that matter, was Bush the first to use language with apocalyptic undertones to describe the stakes in America's confrontations with its enemies. Yet in the days and weeks following 9/11, the president's rhetoric moved beyond the religious and into a new realm of the overtly apocalyptic—using language that, for the second time in as many years, ushered the apocalypse to the center stage of American consciousness. And the American public, primed already for such language by Y2K and its premillennial preoccupations, was more than ready to embrace the new perception that the final showdown was here.

Perhaps fittingly, President Bush first began to use this new mythic language in his remarks at the National Cathedral in Washington, DC, during the National Day of Prayer and Remembrance on September 14. No longer was it sufficient to merely hunt down and punish those responsible for the attacks, the president declared, standing before the altar: "Our responsibility to history is . . . clear: to answer these attacks and *rid the world of evil.*" A tall undertaking, to be sure, especially for a nation grown soporific on the luxuries of consumerism and the distractions of the Internet. But there we were: after one hundred thousand years of human history, it fell upon us (what poor luck!) to destroy the very duality that has defined the human condition for all of time. Fukuyama needn't fret about wasting his life away on video games and martinis at the end of history anymore; instead, the end of history had brought the final grand struggle that had been anticipated by Judeo-Christian thinkers for more than two thousand years.

Bush continued to push ever further the simple and powerful metaphor of apocalyptic showdown to explain the public outbreak of hostilities between the United States and radical Islamists. Regardless of whether one supported or opposed the president's response to 9/11, it's important to note that his framing intrinsically relied on the shared Christian cultural understanding of the apocalypse. Imagine if President Bush had stood up and delivered the same speech that he delivered to the National Cathedral to a nation of people that recognizes the struggle between good and evil as a constant and even desirable characteristic of the world. Without the deep cultural archetype of the apocalypse, and its promise of a final showdown in which good triumphs over evil, the president's framing of the war on terror would, quite literally, have made no sense.

But to Americans, whose religious and national heritage owed a deep debt to the apocalyptic metaphor, and who had been primed for the arrival of the apocalypse (if twenty-one months too early) by the media hysteria surrounding Y2K, the president's rhetoric made perfect sense. Perhaps this *was* the final battle between good and evil; visitation to Todd Strandberg's Rapture Index website suggests that more than a few Americans believed in the days after 9/11 that Armageddon might be here at last. On September 24, 2001—four days after President Bush's address to the joint session of Congress, in which he furthered his apocalyptic metaphor by declaring that the world was either with us or against us in the fight against terrorism—the index hit an all-time high of 182, and Strandberg's web server nearly collapsed as nearly eight million visitors raced to RaptureReady.com to see how the president's words measured up against the yardstick of apocalypse.[16]

The flood of online visitors to the Rapture Index following 9/11 was not the first time Americans had rushed toward an apocalyptic explanation for traumatic events unfolding at home and abroad. In the 1970s, the "no. 1 non-fiction seller of the decade" (as the *New York Times* put it)[17] was Hal Lindsey's *The Late Great Planet Earth*, a paranoid and pun-filled tome that found its way onto the bookshelves of more than fifteen million Americans. A nonfiction (and we use that word loosely) precursor to our decade's pulp-fiction Left Behind series (whose sales jumped 60 percent after 9/11), *The Late Great Planet Earth* found signs of the end times in events from the Yom Kippur War to the energy crisis to the looming threat of nuclear war with the Soviet Union. To a country buffeted by oil shocks, stagflation, Watergate, spiral[ing] [a]nd defeat in Vietnam, *The Late Gr[eat Planet Earth offered a] [s]ort of reverse solace, confirming A[mericans' fears that the wo]rld was coming rapidly undone while offering a cosmological framework for understanding and giving meaning to the bad news. The influence of *The Late Great Planet Earth* was immense. The book nearly single-handedly launched the commercial Christian publishing industry in the United States. And for those who look around and wonder how so many Americans have come to believe that Jesus will soon come to vacuum up the faithful or that violent unrest in the Middle East signals Good News (for the faithful, if not quite for the actual victims of violence in the Middle East), one need only look to Hal Lindsey's bestseller, which arguably introduced the Rapture to more Americans than any other mass-market work in history.

What made the Apocalyptic Decade different from the 1970s—or from any other period of upheaval in American history that has spawned apocalyptic fever—was that the teens and twenty-somethings who had clutched copies of *The Late Great Planet Earth* in the 1970s (and made up a sizable portion of Lindsey's readership) now held the levers of power and media. As journalist Bill Moyers pointed out, "The delusional [was] no longer the marginal. It [had] come in from the fringe, to sit in the seat of power in the Oval Office and in Congress. For the first time in our history, ideology and theology [held] a monopoly of power in Washington."[18] The degree to which President Bush himself believed in the apocalypse is as debated as it is irrelevant; he opened the Oval Office to those who were earnestly apocalyptic, and he used the language of evangelicals to further stoke apocalyptic fervor. A third of American voters went to the polls in 2004 believing that the Rapture was coming, according to one poll;[19] and "forty-five senators and 186 members of the 108th Congress earned 80 to 100 percent approval ratings from the three most influential Christian right advocacy groups."[20] Apocalyptic authors from Jerry B. Jenkins to Joel Rosenberg were frequently invited to the White House and Capitol Hill "to explain the Middle East through the lens of biblical prophecies."[21] To call the apocalyptic marginal or crazy in the 2000s was to call a majority of the US government marginal or crazy (which may well be the case, albeit for different reasons entirely).

Thus, interest in the Rapture Index became a yardstick for measuring apocalypsy itself. *Time* magazine featured the Rapture Index prominently in its cover story on the end times in June of 2002; its popularity was duly noted in the *New York Times*, the *Washington Post*, the *Wall Street Journal*, and in numerous magazine articles and television reports. By 2006, according to the *Los Angeles Times*, "40% of Americans believe[d] that a sequence of events presaging the end times [was] already underway."[22]

Increasingly, Americans turned to the apocalypse as a means of understanding current events—a prism that the media reflected back on the populace. By the summer of 2006, when war broke out between Israel and Hezbollah guerillas in Lebanon, the media's obsession with the end times had morphed from mere (and justifiable) reporting on what fundamentalist Christians believed into a central and recurrent lens through which the media itself interpreted the conflict. In a column for *USA Today*, Gannet News writer Chuck Raasch declared: "You can't look at the headlines these days . . . and not conjure up apocalyptic visions."[23] His fellow journalists clearly agreed and mustered up a series of softball questions for fundamentalist celebrities to help conjure those visions for their audience. "Are we living in the last days?" CNN anchor Kyra Philips earnestly asked her guest in the days following the outbreak of hostilities. Paula Zahn, on the same network, purred in a pre-commercial teaser: "Next in our top story coverage, what does the book of Revelation tell us about what's happening right now in the Middle East?"[24]

Well, frankly, nothing. Nonetheless, during her report, the news ticker beneath Zahn posed the abbreviated question, "The end of the world?" And so, for hundreds of thousands of Americans passing before television sets tuned to CNN in airports and lounges or watching at home, the apocalypse had finally arrived not as a paranoid conspiracy theory but as a catchphrase running along the bottom of the television screen, alongside the NASDAQ and Dow numbers and one-sentence updates from the latest celebrity murder trial. The apocalypse was now firmly ensconced at the center of our discourse. And that Y2K generator out in the garage, many believed, might still come in handy.

THE TIPPING POINT OF CLIMATE CHANGE

Millions of Americans, of course, did not look at the war on terror or the Israeli-Hezbollah conflict as an unfolding of God's plan for the world; they rolled their eyes, muttered in disgust, and angrily flipped the channel in an attempt to escape the cacophony of evangelical apologists and their media courtiers—only to find their own, more scientifically based prophecy of the apocalypse in the alarming reports on the accelerating pace of climate change.

While President Bush maintained throughout his administration that "more evidence" was needed to determine whether human activity was the primary cause of climate change, as the Apocalyptic Decade progressed, evidence that the climate *was* changing became more difficult for the American media and public to ignore. Each successive year brought more dire images from the polar regions and more urgent reports from the world's scientific community. The cataclysmic scenarios of climate change, which only a decade before had seemed confined to a remote and improbable future, appeared to be coming true every time one flipped on the news.

In the spring of 2002, Americans watched reports of the rapid collapse of the Larsen B Ice Shelf in Antarctica. In just thirty-one days, a section of the shelf as large as Rhode Island collapsed into the sea. Barely eighteen months later, reports arrived from the other end of the globe that the Ward Hunt Ice Shelf on the northern coast of Canada, the largest ice shelf in the Arctic, had literally split in two for the first time in at least three thousand years.[25] Each successive spring and summer during the Apocalyptic Decade brought more urgent warnings and vivid evidence of climate change from the extreme north and south—and from points between. Thirty-five thousand Europeans died from a massive heat wave that struck the continent in the summer of 2003; the highest temperatures on record hit dozens of American cities in the summer of 2004, while wildfires raged throughout the Southwest; 2005 was punctuated by the "super-hurricane" season, with Katrina, Rita, and Wilma wreaking unprecedented devastation on the Gulf Coast.

The evidence and the scientific consensus for climate change were under constant amendment as the news consistently worsened. Scientists reported that the earth was at its warmest in 400 years,[26] then amended the comparison to 2,000 years,[27] and then to 12,000 years.[28]

By February of 2006, scientists had declared that we had passed the "tipping point" of climate change: global warming was accelerating far more quickly than anyone had expected just a few years earlier, and the prospect of runaway climate change looked more likely as dangerous feedback loops—such as melting permafrost releasing ever greater concentrations of CO_2 into the atmosphere—began to exacerbate humankind's impact on the planet. "Be worried . . . be very worried," *Time* magazine advised Americans on its April 3, 2006, cover.[29] And millions of Americans—unable to ignore the increasingly dire reports from scientists about the pace of global climate change, or to dismiss the higher temperatures and increasingly odd and extreme weather that they witnessed firsthand on a daily basis—took the advice to heart. We *were* worried, and increasingly so, as the glaciers and ice sheets retreated to reveal a new scenario of imminent apocalypse that rivaled the promise of Rapture and the threat of terrorism on the Right.

AN INCREASING HELPLESSNESS

While a partisan divide emerged over whether global warming or the war on terror was the true apocalyptic threat facing America—or whether the first had been exaggerated to make Al Gore rich or the latter was an excuse to push George Bush's oil-industry agenda—one needn't have been partisan to pick up on the dire American mood. A new phrase had entered the American lexicon—*the tipping point*[30]—and its resonance came from its accurate reflection of our feeling that events were accelerating rapidly beyond our control.

For many Americans, that feeling came crashing ashore alongside Hurricane Katrina at 7 a.m. central daylight time on Monday, August 29, 2005. If global warming and the Rapture could be dismissed as future events, Hurricane Katrina brought the prognostications of future apocalypse and collapse to visceral life—and it was all live on TV.

In the days following Katrina's landfall and the breaching of the levees separating New Orleans from Lake Pontchartrain, Americans watched a city descend into chaos. The "thin veneer of civilization" (to use, as many did at the time, Edgar Rice Burroughs's phrase)[31] disintegrated before our very eyes. Katrina invoked a sense of helplessness in the face of forces beyond our control. We saw public officials weeping on television and threatening to physically attack the president for his inaction, news anchors and reporters visibly disgusted and traumatized on live TV, and an endless stream of images of bodies strewn throughout the flooded city. Many compared the collective experience that we shared through television and the Internet to 9/11, but as traumatized as we were in the days following 9/11, there was a sense that the American government was on top of things, that all available resources were being marshaled to come to the aid of the survivors. In the weeks following 9/11, Americans' faith in government (and the president) soared. With Katrina, both plummeted. If the government couldn't protect American citizens who had been devastated by a threat three hundred miles wide and approaching at a speed of twenty-seven knots, we wondered, how could the government protect its citizens against an epidemic, a dirty bomb, or any of the future apocalyptic scenarios that the media endlessly speculated upon? How could a military capable (as the military spin goes) of delivering precision-guided munitions half a world away at a moment's notice be proven so inept at delivering bottled water to our own backyard? Katrina did more than erode our faith in government preparedness and American invincibility—it effectively killed any remaining notion that we would be Fukuyama's posthistorical Nietzschean Last Man, bored by the velvet comforts of modern technology in a world devoid of struggle.

Katrina would not be the last event of the Apocalyptic Decade to elicit feelings of impotence. The feeling that *the world was coming undone* had crept into the American mind and squatted there, muttering suspiciously. From abroad as well, the images of an unstable world came beaming home: commuter trains blown asunder in Madrid, a double-decker bus peeled open like a sardine can by bombs in London, beheadings and chaos in Iraq, and devastating floods and crippling droughts in Australia and around the world. Solace was rarely found in news closer to home, where the images of orange-jumpsuited prisoners kneeling in the strange sunlit purgatory at Guantanamo Bay seemed emblematic of the trapped helplessness of current events. We watched as the price of energy soared, with gasoline tripling in price from the beginning of the decade, and oil surging to a record high of $147 a barrel in July of 2008. Just months later, Americans awoke to the news that the foundation of our financial system was built on the shifting sands of overleveraged and insolvent banks. The very nature of money came into question. Housing prices plummeted, the stock markets erased a decade of gains, and unemployment surged to 10 percent. Gold soared to more than $1,500 an ounce; the power of the dollar as a global reserve currency was in dispute. Our political system seemed broken, no matter who was elected, and the entrenched partisanship of the decade turned increasing numbers of Americans away from politics. Hope evaporated, like any other campaign promise; the American Dream had turned into a mirage. As the decade came to a close, it seemed that nearly every apocalyptic scenario we had feared—global warming, peak oil, economic collapse, environmental disaster—had taken place. The apocalypse was to be expected as a matter of course.

We had entered the Apocalyptic Decade as a rich, powerful,

and just nation; we left the decade far poorer, both in material wealth and in optimism, with our confidence shaken and our global image badly tarnished. How quickly we had forgotten the golden optimism of the 1990s and Fukuyama's vision of our elite and untouchable status as the victors of history. History wasn't over; history appeared to be accelerating—it was bearing down on us and threatening to bury us. As the second decade of the twenty-first century arrived, the news just seemed to get worse. The Deepwater Horizon oil platform exploded in the Gulf of Mexico, leaking more than five million barrels of oil for three helpless and frustrating months. The price of oil, which had crashed to just $37 per barrel in 2009, surged back above $100 by 2011, threatening to strangle any hope of an economic recovery. The price of food soared, leading to smaller packages in American supermarkets and revolutions in the Arab street.[32] Nothing seemed sustainable; surely, we told ourselves, at some moment it would all come crashing down. On March 28, 2011, as the world anxiously awaited the attempts of Japanese workers to halt a full meltdown in four reactors at the Fukushima nuclear plant, *Newsweek* released a "special double issue" featuring a foreboding, black-and-white tidal wave over which bold, blood-red letters blared the title "Apocalypse Now." The subtitle of the issue perfectly captured the public's growing sense of overwhelmed and exasperated helplessness: "Tsunamis. Earthquakes. Nuclear Meltdowns. Revolutions. Economies on the Brink. What the #@%! Is Next?"

But for millions of Americans, accustomed as we were after a long decade of disaster and disappointment to apocalyptic thinking and expectation, the answer to the question had been formulated before it had even been asked.

What was next was December 21, 2012.

CHAPTER 2

THE PAST IS A FOREIGN COUNTRY

No one can agree on precisely what will happen. Some believe a massive solar flare will erupt from the Sun; eight minutes later, a force equivalent to a billion atomic bombs will strike the Earth's atmosphere, incinerating every satellite in orbit and plunging the world into primitive chaos. Others believe the Earth will experience a sudden reversal of the poles, an event that will weaken the Earth's protective magnetic field and expose each and every one of us to the direct radiation of the sun; imagine popcorn in a microwave, and you as a kernel. Some say that a mysterious Planet X will emerge from its hiding place behind the Sun and pass so close to our own planet that the Earth will be knocked off its axis, sending the oceans surging around the globe and devastating human civilization in a series of tsunamis. Some believe we don't need an astronomical event to wipe out the modern world; the eruption of the Yellowstone supervolcano, or a series of global earthquakes, wars, or famines should do the trick. Still others reject any cataclysm whatsoever, believing instead that the end of the 26,000-year precession of the equinoxes will bring the Earth and Sun into perfect alignment with a black hole at the center of our galaxy, producing (through indeterminate means; the exact details have yet to be worked out) a sudden shift in human consciousness,

41

which will be identifiable by a sharp spike in sales of books by Carlos Castaneda.

Though few can agree on *what* will happen, many agree that *something* will take place on December 21, 2012—the day that the ancient Mayans supposedly prophesied the end of our world. According to various New Age and neo-Christian thinkers and astrologers, the primary reason the ancient Mayans built one of the grandest civilizations of the Mesoamerican world—with its complex calendars, advanced astronomy, and the only fully developed written language in the Americas before Columbus—was not simply because they were curious about the world and wanted to communicate their understanding and experience of it, but because they were obsessed with *us*. A deluge of books and documentaries about 2012 insist that the Mayans were apocalyptic visionaries who spent their days thinking up complex ways to warn us that some terrible catastrophe or some quantum shift in consciousness is headed our way in the very near future. As the psychedelic thinker Terence McKenna has written, "It was *our time* that fascinated the Maya. It was toward *our time* that they cast their ecstatic gaze."[1]

The problem is that none of this is true, and the Mayan doomsday industry has revealed more about our own historical narcissism (that great cultural contribution of the Boomer generation) than it has about the beliefs of the ancient Mayans. It must be pointed out—must it be pointed out?—that the Mayans weren't, in fact, obsessed with us. Nor is there any evidence that the end of the thirteenth baktun in the Mayan Long Count calendar—the day that many have correlated (though perhaps incorrectly) with December 21, 2012—held any more significance to the ancient Mayans than the beginning of the first baktun.

The society whose "ecstatic gaze" is focused on the apocalypse is ours, not the Mayans'.[2] Reeling from the effects and images of the Apocalyptic Decade, we're so intent on looking forward to the Big One that we find ourselves also looking behind us to past civilizations for clues as to when the Big One might come. Remember the Hopi? In the early 1960s, a white anthropologist by the name of Frank Waters visited the Hopi and revealed that they had a secret prophecy for the end of the world—and that eight of the nine criteria for that end had already been met.[3] Whether Waters's account is accurate (and many Hopi dispute it) or exploitative, the fact that he heard the story in the early 1960s tells us nothing about what ancient peoples believed. After all, the myths of contemporary native peoples don't exist in isolation from the modern world. It's no surprise that after five hundred years of Christian influence, the decimation of Hopi culture, and the arrival of the nuclear age that even the Hopi would have caught the apocalyptic bug.

Instead of apocalyptic visionaries, the Mayans, like the Hopis before them, are simply the latest in a long list of ancient cultures upon whom we've projected our own Western apocalyptic expectations, arming them with beliefs they didn't have—and that didn't exist in the ancient world.

More history is in order.

THE WAY THINGS WERE WHEN THE WORLD WAS YOUNG

Because we're surrounded by apocalyptic belief and rhetoric today, it's easy to assume that how and when the world will end has always been a central question of the human experience. Indeed, we frequently turn to that assumption as a means of dismissing our own apocalyptic anxiety whenever it begins to make us uncomfortable. "People have always believed in the end of the world," we say, as though our anxiety can be dismissed simply by pointing to its imagined historical consistency. But it's a fundamental error of logic to believe that something that is omnipresent now must have been equally omnipresent in the past. It's like seeing a freeway jammed with cars and assuming that because so many people rely on cars on a daily basis, the automobile must have always been a part of human culture. That such logic is flawed is obvious when it is applied to the automobile, of course, but it's a logic that many people apply to the history of apocalypse.

In fact, there is nothing innately human about obsessing over the end of the world as we do today. There is nothing in our biology that says we must believe the end of the world is imminent, nothing in our genes that compels us to feel such dread for what the future may hold. From the perspective of pure reason, as the millennialist scholar Stephen O'Leary has pointed out, eschatology—the study of last things—is not a necessary idea.[4] To understand this fully, and to get at the root of where our idea of apocalypse originated, we must widen our frame of reference to capture more than the sliver of human experience that we commonly think of as history. It's not enough to start merely with the rise of Christianity, or the advent of civilization, or even the dawn of agriculture. Rather, we must widen our frame of reference until it contains as much of the more than one hundred thousand years of human experience as possible, stripping away centuries of our Enlightenment thinking and millennia of our religious assumptions, taking a hammer to the very foundations of the way we view the world. We admit this is not an easy task; most of us can't even get the pop song we heard on the radio this morning out of our heads, much less the parameters of assumption that define the Western mind. Yet we must try, because the story of how the apocalypse came into being is not merely a story about how humanity has thought about the end of the world—it's a story about our fundamental understanding of meaning in the universe.

With our camera pulled back to capture as panoramic a view of human history as possible, we can see that there was indeed a time when people did not think apocalyptically—in fact, a very long time, for at least one hundred thousand years of human history. The idea of apocalypse relies on a series of assumptions about the universe that did not even exist for traditional humanity. Those assumptions include a linear view of time, a belief in the importance of history, and the expectation of a final, predestined battle between good and evil. People must first think that history is important before they can care about how it will end; until that sense of historical consciousness developed, the apocalypse as an idea could not—and did not—exist.[5]

Our understanding of time is fundamental to the way we perceive the world. For nearly all of human history, humanity has held a circular view of time—the understanding that the universe goes through periods of birth, renewal, decay, and death; periods that repeat endlessly, just as the seasons and diurnal cycles repeat themselves endlessly. This understanding of circular time arose, quite naturally, from humanity's observations of the seasons; of the movement of the planets and the moon; and of the life cycles of humans, plants, and animals. From an evolutionary perspective, it makes perfect sense that humanity's conception of time would arise from the observations of the world in which our consciousness evolved. The template for our earliest cosmology was manifest in the first blooming of the spring flowers, in the falling of the forest leaves with the first cold nights of autumn, in the deaths of animals, in the migration of game. Nature provided the basis for belief in an eternal, if ever-changing, world; one predator might disappear from the forest, but another would return to fulfill its role. Thus, for most of human history, humanity believed without doubt that the world eternally created and re-created itself.

Yet to conceive of the idea of circular time as little more than a metaphor for seasons and diurnal cycles is to miss the critical component of the traditional view of circular time: that there was a *center* to that circle and that center was *myth*.

Today we often use the word *myth* to describe the opposite of reality, as something unreal, but for the traditional mind, the myth at the center of the circle of time *was* reality. It was in the center of this circle that the gods lived, it was in the center of this circle that the stories of creation were constantly unfolding, and it was upon creation and the beginnings of the world that humanity's gaze was focused. For traditional people, creation was not some discrete moment in the past; it was an ongoing event that occurred eternally in the mythical realm of the gods. Whatever humans did was simply a replication, a ritual reenactment, of what the gods had done or were doing.[6] If a person fell ill, it was because a god had fallen ill. When someone planted a crop, he or she was simply replicating the moment when the gods themselves had first planted crops in the stories of creation. There was nothing new under the sun, nothing that humankind could do that the gods themselves had not already done. The wheel of time spun, to be sure, and the particulars changed—the seasons, the animals, the individual humans—but those particulars acquired their meaning only to the extent that they repeated the larger mythical archetypes that existed at the center of the circle. The cyclical view of time was not just a different way of looking at history, as we might presume—it was in fact *ahistorical*.[7]

This difference between the traditional view of cyclical time, centered in myth, and our own linear view of time as the unfolding of history can hardly be overstated. To sum it up, the "chief difference between archaic man and modern . . . is that the former feels indissolubly connected with the cosmos and its rhythms while the latter insists he is connected only to History."[8] This sounds rather romantic—who wouldn't prefer to feel connected to the cosmos rather than some dreary Monday in, say, 1989?—but the point is that traditional peoples lacked a historical consciousness as we understand it. Our sense of history as the place where things *happen*—where God intervenes, or does not, and where man makes a name for himself, or does not—is profoundly different from what people have believed for nearly all of human history.

Today, we rarely place value on the ritual repetition of archetypal forms. Instead, the stories we tell ourselves place the highest value on things that are unusual, unique, and groundbreaking—or, in a word, *historic*. We are "unique individuals," we collectively tell ourselves, at a "new point in history" that has "never come before." We value the expressions of our own individuality and a pioneering and entrepreneurial spirit that "throws out the old" and finds "a new way of doing things." We don't celebrate the traditional, we celebrate the novel—no matter how trivial or commercial the breakthrough. (Invent a successful iPhone® app and you'll be heralded as a genius.) We focus so much on unique storylines that nowadays it is fashionable in marketing and public relations to imply that "narrative" has always been the predominant metaphor for human life.

But in the traditional worldview, life wasn't a narrative with a beginning, middle, and end; life was a rhythm—and the beat was written by gods rather than human ingenuity. The traditional worldview actively denied meaning to those unique events that happened in what we would call history. For traditional people, there was no such thing as novelty; they acknowledged "no act [that had] not been previously posited and lived by someone else."9

Yet traditional people didn't merely believe different things than we believe; the focus of their belief system was different from ours. Their focus was on the beginning of the world, not on the end of it. Traditional societies focused on *how things came to be.* Endings in traditional mythology were often little more than an afterthought, if they existed at all—an extension of the more important story of creation. The presumption that a beginning needs an end to give a story meaning is a tautology of linear thinking, not a requisite of the human condition. In the traditional circular view, humanity's gaze was fixed on the creative center, rather than on the end. Any ending would only result in rebirth and the recurrence of the creative cycle—so why be obsessed with it? To traditional people, endings were not nearly as important as creation itself, and creation mythology sought to explain how the world is, rather than how things would be later.

Like traditional people, of course, we, too, have creation myths and stories that explain how the world began. Yet whether those stories are taken from Genesis or from scientific journals, whether we believe God created the earth in seven days or that the first single-celled organisms appeared on earth three billion years ago, our focus rarely stays on creation. From our vantage point, the past is nearly always a mere prelude to the real focus of our curiosity: THE END. We read Genesis quickly to get to Revelation. Like children who skip ahead in a book, our gaze is always most interested not in how things came to be as they are, but in *how it all ends up*.

Eschatology is simply the study of last things. Yet eschatological myths can exist to address a wide range of subjects, from mortality, to what happens in the afterlife, to understanding how previous worlds ended or how this one might fade away. An eschatology needn't be concerned with the end of history, or the meaning of history, or the triumph of good over evil, or even the final end of time or the total destruction of the world—all of which are questions that our modern idea of apocalypse seeks to answer. To assume that all eschatologies are apocalyptic gets it backward: the apocalypse is simply one version of end-times mythology—one that is fixated on an ultimate, final ending. The apocalypse is eschatology in overdrive. Yet when held up against the whole of human history, the apocalyptic notion that the world will end once and for all—and in its ending validate our own worldview—is a remarkably recent development. We mistakenly project this apocalyptic anxiety onto other cultures, forgetting that they had no need to consider such things, for they were concerned with *how things came to be* rather than *how things will end*.

In fact, not only did many other cultures in the past lack an apocalyptic eschatology—some had no eschatological myths whatsoever. Although we find the question of how the world might end endlessly fascinating and worthy of a Memorial Day matinee, some cultures just didn't give any thought at all to the idea that a volcano might erupt beneath Los Angeles (to take one such movie scenario as an example) to herald the end of human history. For instance, the Cherokee oral tradition has no story that explicitly prophesies or expects the end of the world.[10] The contemporary Amondawa people who live in the Amazon similarly have no story for the end of time—because they have no concept of time "as something that can be measured, counted, or talked about in the abstract."[11] Other tribes throughout the world similarly lack a consideration of a final end to the world.

When traditional cultures did consider endings, such endings were usually part of a larger creation story. A story from the Sioux serves as a good example. After going to great lengths to describe the creation of the present world (there were two worlds before this one, according to the myth, but both were destroyed by the Creating Power when he found people misbehaving), the Creating Power tells his people that if they "learn how to live in peace with each other and with other living things . . . then all will be well. But if you make this world bad and ugly, then I will destroy this world too. It's up to you." Before resting, the Creating Power observes that "someday there might be a fourth world."[12]

This Sioux story is typical of cyclical stories of destruction and renewal that can be found throughout the Americas and across the world—including in the cosmology of the Mayans—but it is not apocalyptic. At first glance we might see shadows of the apocalypse in the destruction of the world, but in the Sioux story, the end of the world is neither predestined nor necessarily final. The Sioux story is full of *ifs* and *mights*. Indeed, the story allows humans to forestall the end of the world indefinitely. At best, it's an *Apocalypse Maybe*—which is not really an apocalypse at all. In the Judeo-Christian apocalypse, "there is no suggestion . . . that human beings can, by their obedience or disobedience, affect the shape of things to come. The future is already determined . . . its course is already inscribed in a heavenly book."[13] Although we tend to fixate on the mere mention of a destructive ending in the story, for the Sioux, the moments of destruction are referenced only as an aside in explaining how the world came to be and as an addendum to the larger creation myth. For the traditional listener, the destruction of the world is a dramatic device designed to enforce proper behavior; it's not the point of the play. The point of the play is creation, and renewal is always a possibility.

Such traditions describing the past destruction of the world as a moral cautionary tale are not confined to native North Americans. The Great Flood, for example, makes an appearance in mythic traditions throughout the world, from precontact Native Americans to the Mesopotamian *Epic of Gilgamesh*, and from the Old Testament story of Noah to the classical obsession with the lost city of Atlantis. But fire and flood do not an apocalypse make. In these stories that sound apocalyptic, as in the Sioux myth, the world does not cease to exist. Time doesn't end; the world simply begins again. Whether by fire, flood, or ice, the great cataclysms of ancient mythology always provide the means for the world to begin anew—to focus again on creation.

For the traditional person, creation and destruction coexisted in the sacred center of time, with chaos and order in an eternal, perfectly balanced embrace. In the traditional view, nations rose and fell, people lived and died, yet everything was constantly reborn. Endings were inevitable and constant and unknowable, but not final—and most importantly, not imminent.

The rise of agriculture and the earliest civilizations did little to alter this view of a fundamentally stable, balanced, and endless universe. Although a shift took place from animism and shamanism to a belief in mother goddesses during the first nine thousand years of practicing agriculture, and then to a belief in a pantheon of gods ruling from the heavens during the first three thousand years of civilization,[14] humanity maintained throughout both shifts its belief in cyclical time, in the mythic center, and in a stable cosmos balanced by periods of generation and regeneration.

Apocalyptic expectation of a final end, to put it simply, is not an idea that coincided with the development of civilization. Two of the earliest societies in the cradle of civilization—the Sumerians and the Egyptians—show us how civilization and prehistoric beliefs were able to coexist for several thousand years.

More than five thousand years before Christ, at the beginning of the Bronze Age, humans began to live in the first cities of the world in southern Mesopotamia, between the Tigris and Euphrates Rivers in modern-day Iraq. Archaeological evidence shows that at the beginning of historic time (and with the advent of writing) around 3000 BCE, these Sumerian-speaking peoples held a worldview that was little changed from the one held by their prehistoric forebears.[15] As with traditional humans, Sumerians believed that their actions were reenactments of the mythical gestures that the gods themselves had performed at the beginning of the world. (That the mythical act was now digging an irrigation ditch instead of going on a hunt didn't appreciably change the sacredness of the act.) So, too, did the Sumerians believe, as pre-civilized people had believed, that the gods were always present, not only metaphorically at the sacred center of time but literally at the very center of the new Sumerian city-states. Each of the dozen cities that arose in ancient Sumer by 2500 BCE had its own patron god who "lived" in a temple that the people of each city built for him—temples that would by the sixth century BCE become the famous ziggurats of the Babylonian and Assyrian Empires.[16] The temples, Sumerians believed, were not designed from human inspiration; their very measurements were prescribed by the gods, who had built the first temples for themselves. Thus, in building and rebuilding the temples within their cities, the Sumerians could repeat the very gestures that the gods had made at the beginning of time.[17]

Like the Sumerians, the Egyptians believed that the world was ordered and stable, a worldview summed up in their belief in *ma'at*, "a principle of order so all-embracing," historian Norman Cohn tells us, that it "governed every aspect of existence," from how the sun moved through the sky to how people interacted with each other to when rituals were performed by the Egyptian priests. *Ma'at* was in a state of constantly shifting balance with its mirror opposite, *isfet*, or chaos—the yin and yang of the Egyptian world.[18]

It's tempting to look at such ancient beliefs of order and chaos balanced in a shifting embrace and to compare them to the Judeo-Christian belief in good and evil. Though the dualistic worldview of the Hebrews would be greatly influenced by the Egyptian worldview, there is a critical difference. For the Egyptians, the final victory over chaos by order was never meant to arrive. There was never any expectation of a future in which the threat of chaos, which defined the edges of the ordered world, would be eradicated. An apocalypse, a final end to the struggle between order and chaos, was as unimaginable to the Egyptian mind as was the end of the kingdom.[19]

Along with the isolation that Egypt enjoyed until late in its history, protected as it was by vast deserts and the Red and Mediterranean Seas, the Egyptian faith in the stability of the world allowed Egyptian civilization to flourish for nearly 2,500 years, until successive invasions by the Persians and Alexander the Great finally weakened Egypt to the point that it could be absorbed into the Roman Empire, merely thirty years before the birth of Christ. (Most ancient civilizations rarely flourished for more than three centuries.)

The Egyptian faith in the permanence of the world is nowhere more evident than in the greatest achievement of antiquity: the pyramids. Consider as a measurement of that faith the stones of the Great Pyramids—weighing more than two and a half tons each—and compare them to the flimsy materials with which we build our current McMansions, which one might consider monuments not just to cheap labor and subpar materials but to our own belief that the world is disintegrating. More than mere monuments to dead kings, the pyramids stand as a continuous testament to the ancient world's faith in a stable and permanent cosmos.

To insist that prehistoric and early civilized peoples anticipated the end of the world as we do is to arm them with intellectual concepts that did not yet exist or, more accurately, were actively rejected by the fundamental constructs of their worldview. While we perceive time in a linear manner, they believed it was cyclical; while we believe that history gives the world meaning, they believed myth and ritual gave the world meaning; while many of us believe good and evil will one day face a final showdown, they believed that order and chaos were in an eternal, if shifting, balance. Much of that ancient worldview still remains, of course; we still experience cyclical time in nature and through our seasonal holidays and rituals. Yet simply because we find familiarity in looking back at the ancient past doesn't mean that the ancients themselves, if they could have looked forward at us, would have experienced a similar sense of recognition.

The past is a foreign country, as L. P. Hartley wrote; they do things differently there.[20]

A WORLD FRESH IN RUINS

If the rise of the earliest civilizations did little to alter the traditional view of time and the cosmos, then what caused people to turn their focus from eternal creation and begin to develop an understanding of history? Here's a story that might help us begin to formulate an answer.

When the Indo-Aryans, after centuries of marauding on the Russian steppes, first descended into the Indus valley in their chariots around 1500 BCE, they discovered one of the greatest and most fertile riverine valleys of the world populated by scattered villages of people living in primitive conditions.[21] Like the Egyptians, the Indo-Aryans brought with them a view of a stable cosmology, in which every action they performed was a reflection of the actions originally done by the gods, in which there was nothing new under the sun. So they were stunned, no doubt, to find between the scattered villages the abandoned cities of a once-great civilization. Riding their chariots between the crumbling buildings of the devastated cities, they would have seen things they had never before imagined. Streets laid out at perfect right angles. Stone tablets bearing strange figures that, we know today, symbolized a system of weights and measures using the decimal system. From inside the houses, the viaducts of the world's first indoor sanitation system snaked outward. In the dirt between the abandoned houses, they may have found a bronze figurine of a dancing girl, a figurine so delicate and beautiful—an impassioned young woman with a long slender arm resting insouciantly on a jutting hip, awaiting a suitor's next request to dance—that it would take more than 1,200 years before the Greeks would rediscover the figurine's rules of proportion and match its artistry.[22]

The Indo-Aryans had encountered the remnants of the Harappan civilization in modern-day Pakistan. They were neither the first nor the last to encounter evidence of a once-Golden Age. Across the world, the ruins of past civilizations were piling up everywhere, and these ruins presented not just a mystery but a crisis of metaphysics. Without ruins, perhaps, there is little to prompt the human mind to even conceive of history beyond the archetypes of the ancestors. Yet if past civilizations had not lasted forever, then perhaps the mythical realm no longer fully explained all that humans encountered in the world. Propelled by the intersecting advances of astronomy, mathematics, and writing, and beginning no later than 700 BCE (and probably as early as 2000–1500 BCE), the civilized world began to turn away from the sacred center of eternal creation to focus instead on the turning wheel of time itself. Time, the civilized world slowly came to understand, could be measured. A new vision of cosmology—what we might call the Declining Ages of Man—emerged.[23]

What was this new idea of the Declining Ages of Man? Picture the traditional wheel of circular time, divided into four quadrants and spinning in a clockwise direction. The Vedic Indians (as the Indo-Aryans who settled in the Indus valley became known) imagined that the upper-left quadrant of the wheel represented the first yuga, or age, known as the Satya. The Satya is the age of truth, a period ruled by the gods, where humans live for four thousand years in a state of equality and spiritual bliss. The second yuga, the Treta, is on the upper right of our wheel of time; during this era, mental powers have replaced spiritual powers, and humans—not the gods—rule the world. Beginning to descend to the bottom of the circle, on the lower right, we enter the Dvapara Yuga, the age of arcana, a period when science flourishes but people themselves cease to be truthful, and when disease and ailments begin to torment humanity. In the final age—the Kali Yuga, the age most Hindus believe we are now in—we are at the lowest possible point of the circle. It is a dark age, a time when people are farthest from spiritual truth, when famines strike nations and tragedies strike families.[24] It is a time of murder, lust, and despair—a time we might well recognize as our own.

According to the sacred texts of Hinduism, as well as early Vedic astronomy, each yuga, or each declining age of humans, has a precise length. The entire cycle—the period from the creation of the world until its destruction—is believed to last 4,320,000 years. The Kali Yuga, the decrepit age that most Hindus believe we are now in, will last 432,000 years. (Unfortunately for us, the Kali Yuga probably began in 3102 BCE, which means we've got another 426,890 years before things measurably improve.) At the end of the Kali Yuga, Hindus believe, the world will be consumed by fire and flood, and then the world will rest for a time in the form of the primordial ocean from which everything first originated, before the entire cycle begins anew.[25]

The Vedic tribes began to conceive of the yugas in the Brahmanas, written between 800 and 600 BCE, and they perfected the idea in the Puranas, written between 320 and 500 CE. Thanks to this long written history, the Vedic tradition provides a clear window into the development of the idea of the Declining Ages of Man. That doesn't mean that the idea originated in the Indus valley; indeed, no one knows for certain where the idea of successive ages of humankind first developed. There is little doubt that it captured the imagination of humankind, however, for it appears nearly contemporaneously, beginning around 700 BCE, in a period known as the Axial Age, in the Vedic, Persian, and Greco-

Roman worlds, and the idea soon takes hold in the dynastic view of history of the Chinese culture that was then extending far beyond the Huang He-Yangtze valley.[26] The concept of the successive ages also appears, later and most famously, among the Mayan civilization in Central America and, later still, among the Hopi and other tribes of North America. And in Persia, the Declining Ages of Man would provide the foundation for an even more radical conception of time and history.[27]

Within Western civilization, we first find evidence of the Declining Ages of Man in the Greek poet Hesiod's *Works and Days*, a long poem written around 700 BCE that describes the history of Greek mythical cosmology. In *Works and Days*, Hesiod recounts the Golden Age, when humans lived among the gods; which was followed by the Silver Age, when Zeus ruled the world; the Bronze Age (a time of war); and the Heroic Age, when the Trojan War took place. Humanity, according to Hesiod, now lives in the Iron Age, and it's not that great a place to be: children disrespect their parents, corruption runs rampant, and humankind is condemned to a life of misery.[28]

More commonly than Hesiod's description of five ages, the cycle of ages was typically broken down into four ages in most of the ancient world. The Roman poet Ovid put down the Roman vision of four ages in his poem *Metamorphoses*, written around 8 CE. The Persians believed that the 12,000 years of earth's existence could be broken down into four eras of 3,000 years each.[29] In Babylon, beginning in the seventh century BCE, astrology began to flourish, and the concept of the "Great Year" divided into four seasons became well known across the Hellenistic world. Elsewhere in the civilized world—among the Jainist revolutionaries of sixth-century BCE India and among the Chinese conception of dynastic cycles, for example—history was soon divided into twelve recurring ages.[30]

What is important to note in this "avalanche of figures"[31] is not the specificity of each culture's division of the world into four or twelve successive ages, nor the perceived length of those ages. What is significant is that this measurement of the ages marks the ancient civilized world's first great contribution to our eschatological heritage: the idea of measured ages, with each age in a state of perpetual decline—a decline that could only be halted by the destruction of the current age (or world) and the birth of a new one.

But the Declining Ages of Man is not yet apocalyptic. Although it is tempting to try to find similarities between the Hindu period of destruction and the Christian account of apocalypse as rendered in the book of Revelation—fiery brimstone falls from the sky, the world is destroyed by flood, and all sorts of mayhem is visited on the world—these similarities are cinematic rather than theological. The annihilation of the world at the end of the Kali Yuga is not properly the final end, for the cycle of creation begins anew for another period of 4,320,000 years. In the Vedic tradition, this repetition of the creation, destruction, and new creation continues indefinitely, while in the Christian tradition, the return of Christ can happen only once, and the only other world available is a heavenly one, not an earthly one.

Nor can the return of the Satya Yuga properly be compared to the thousand-year reign of Christ that follows the Christian vision of Armageddon. The next Satya Yuga, like all the Satya Yugas that came before it and all those that will come after it, is destined to end as well; after that, cyclical history will continue ad infinitum. Nor does the Vedic annihilation of the world have much, if anything, to do with the immortality of human beings, as the Chris-

tian vision of Armageddon does. The Hindu belief in reincarna-
tion, after all, holds that death is but a brief intermission between
an endlessly repeating succession of rebirths. In the Vedic and
modern Hindu traditions, there is no completion to history, nor
any universal last judgment—ideas necessary for our modern secular vision of apocalypse. Hinduism lacked (and today still lacks)
any consideration of a final, cosmological end to the world.[32] As it
was for traditional societies, in the vision of the Declining Ages of
Man, the end is never final or complete but recurring. When the
end of the world is imagined, it is not *the* end but *an* end.

ANCIENT MAYANS AND MODERN MYSTICS

When New Age and neo-religious thinkers insist that the measurements and prophesies of ancient cultures bear influence over contemporary events, or that ancient cultures possessed some esoteric
knowledge that they felt compelled to preserve for us, they make
the basic mistake of allowing their own cultural bias to cloud their
view of history. Nowhere is this mistake—this basic misunder-
standing of what the ancients believed and the attempt to wed
those beliefs to our own daydreams of the end—more apparent
than in the contemporary obsession with, and misinterpretation of,
the end of the Mayan Long Count calendar on December 21, 2012.

   The Mayans—whose civilization reached its zenith on the
Yucatán Peninsula from about 250 to 900 CE—were profoundly
accomplished in math and astronomy and developed a complex
series of calendars in the sixth century BCE. These included a ceremonial calendar, a solar calendar for civic functions, a lunar cal-

endar, a calendar to monitor the conjunctions of Venus (every 584 days), and an 819-day calendar that was associated with various deities.[33] By combining the 260-day ceremonial calendar with the 365-day solar calendar, the Mayans created a cycle that repeated itself every 52 years; the completion of each 52-year cycle was marked by grand ceremonies and the forgiveness of debts (not unlike the Hebrew Jubilee). To measure periods longer than 52 years, the Mayans possessed a calendar that they called the Long Count, which represented a period of 5,125 years as counted through 13 baktuns of 144,000 days, or approximately 394 years.[34]

How did all these complex calculations fit into the Mayan cosmology? We hardly know. Our knowledge of ancient Mayan belief is severely limited; when the Spanish conquistadors and priests arrived in the Yucatán Peninsula in the sixteenth century, they burned all but three of the vast collection of Mayan codices, or books, that had recorded Mayan history and beliefs for at least eight hundred years. Part of what we do know can be deduced from the legends of the *Popol Vuh*, a phonetic transcription of the mythological narratives of the K'iche' Maya of Guatemala. The creation myths within the *Popol Vuh* reflect the Mayan beliefs in recurring cycles of destruction and renewal, as well as the widely held Mesoamerican belief in successive suns, which, some argue, the Mayans believed lasted the length of the Long Count calendar, or 5,125 years.[35] Mayan glyphs show that the current sun represents the fifth age of the world in a grand, recurring cycle. And the final page of the famous Dresden Codex—one of the three Mayan codices to survive the conquistadors—illustrates the cataclysmic destruction that is prophesied to come at the end of the current sun.

Yet there is no incontrovertible evidence that the winter solstice in 2012 accurately correlates with the fifth and final sun of the

Mayan Great Cycle. That date was chosen by scholars of Mayan history in the 1930s, who needed a standard correlation between the Mayan Long Count calendar and our own Gregorian calendar in order to compare their academic notes; they may well have gotten the math wrong. Some believe that the Long Count ended on October 28, 2011; others predict March 31, 2013.[36] Still others believe that what the Long Count was measuring was not the beginning and the end of the current world but one-quarter of the precession of the equinoxes. Perhaps we are simply confusing the Mayan belief in multiple worlds with their measurement of the Platonic or Great Year, that 26,000-year wobble of the Earth on its axis that has been observed by numerous societies since before the Axial Age.[37]

Whichever date correlates with the end of the Great Cycle, however, the question remains: Did the Mayans believe that the end of the Long Count represented the end of the world? It's unlikely—and not a belief held by modern-day descendants of the Maya. When we put the few available disparate records and clues together and remove our own apocalyptic goggles, we see in the ancient Mayan viewpoint a cosmological vision that could be found throughout the Hellenistic and Vedic worlds in late antiquity: vast, recurring ages, measured through astronomy, that last thousands of years; periodic, cataclysmic destruction and renewal marking the point of demarcation between the ages; and an enduring attachment, maintained through ritual and religion, to the cycles of myth from which prehistoric humanity had found its meaning. Mayan cosmology was, in a sense, mundanely typical for a late-antiquity civilization, though it flourished later than similar cosmologies in the Indus valley or between the Tigris and Euphrates Rivers. There's very little evidence to suggest that the end of the Long Count represented for them the end of the world—and quite a bit that suggests it didn't represent the end. A panel at the Temple of the Inscriptions in Palenque, for example, bears a date that correlates to October 21, 4772 CE[38]—just one of many inscriptions suggesting that the ancient Mayans didn't expect the world to go kaput in 2012 any more than you'd expect the world to end because your desk calendar reads December 31. Calendars repeat, after all, even when they come to their final number, no matter whether that number is 365 days or 5,125 years. The Mayans may as likely have expected one heck of a New Year's party at the conclusion of the Long Count as they expected the end of the world.

Like most cultures of late antiquity, the ancient Mayans believed that the current age marked the last declining age of the world—but it was the last declining age in a circle. And as with most ancient cultures, the Mayans placed themselves in the midst of that declining age rather than at the end of it.[39] Ask a contemporary yogi when the Kali Yuga will end, and he or she will tell you: not for thousands of years. Ask a Buddhist when the current kalpa will end, and he or she will probably look at you blankly for some time before replying (if replying at all): a few billion years. So, too, did the Mayans, at the height of their civilization, place the end of their age safely some 1,500 years into the future, well beyond the perspective of their collective experience.

That hardly makes the ancient Mayans the modern apocalyptic visionaries they are so often portrayed to be. After all, it's not a particularly bold or prophetic statement to claim that in 1,500 years, our world and culture will not exist, some other world and culture will be coming into being, and the transition between those worlds will be cataclysmic and difficult. It's not particularly remarkable that the Mayans—as with the Hindus and Jainists and Babylonians, all of whom believed in cyclical, declining ages—recognized that their time on earth was not permanent but rather was just a passing spoke in a larger spinning wheel of cosmological time. They understood that an end of their way of life would come, made some calculations based on astronomical observation about when that end would arrive, and deduced from those calculations that the end was very far away. The things that seemed so distant to them, from our perspective, are now here; but that does not mean they shared our preoccupation with the end of the world, any more than we are preoccupied with the eventual end of the sun, which our astronomy tells us with absolute certitude will happen in about five billion years.

* * *

It took thousands of years, and the rise of writing, astronomy, and mathematics, for humanity to begin to develop a more measured relationship to time and to begin to wrestle with the problem of historicity. In those earliest days of historical consciousness, history and myth coexisted. Indeed, history was still perceived as an aid to myth, rather than its replacement. The cosmogenic cycle and the Declining Ages of Man helped humanity better understand the mythical world of the gods and the ages of creation and renewal, which is why the earliest civilizations always arranged their visions of historical time into huge, thousands-of-years ages, reflecting the vast scope of their cosmology.

Yet this interpretation of the world moving through a cycle of declining ages set the stage for a new, epochal understanding of time. In the contemporary Middle East, still dwelling in the riverine valleys that had been the cradles of civilization, humans could see around them the ruins of previous civilizations that had built great cities; they could experience the tides of empires as they swept across Mesopotamia; and they began to accumulate a written record of those who came before them, a record that slowly began to compete with the mythic repetition of the sacred as a source for human meaning.

It is into this new, evolving concept of the world, at a time when humanity was first groping toward a sense of history and periodicity, when we were first reimagining our place in the world as closer to the end of an age than to the eternal beginnings of creation—in the later hours of the world's afternoon—that the Judaic tradition arrived on the scene.

CHAPTER 3

THE EVOLUTION OF
THE APOCALYPSE

Imagine the apocalypse as a virus.

Without a host, a virus is little more than a harmless assemblage of RNA or DNA wrapped in a protective coat of proteins. It is only when a virus finds a host cell that it is capable of changing itself and its surroundings. The virus that causes the common cold is essentially inert—scientists debate whether to even call it a living organism—until it attaches itself to receptors on the surface of cells in the human nose and throat. Once attached to the receptor, the virus may lay dormant for a time, but eventually it inserts its genetic information into the host cell, altering the host cell and producing a systemic infection. Because this is merely the common cold, of course, our bodies eventually respond to the virus by releasing antibodies to counteract it, and soon we are well again. But other viruses, such as influenza, are more serious and sinister; they can sweep through large populations of people quickly, altering themselves and evolving as they spread, killing off one host even while jumping to another, and then disappearing, almost as quickly as they had broken out, only to return again the following season, stronger and more virulent than before. But without access to a host, the virus does not exist.

So, too, the idea of the apocalypse could not exist until we had developed our understanding of history as a meaningful place where important stuff happens. For more than one hundred thousand years, humankind had imagined that the source of meaning in the universe came from the sacred center of myth—a wellspring of creation and stability. To the extent that traditional societies possessed eschatological myths, such myths served as merely a coda to a nearly all-consuming interest in the world's creation. The virus of the apocalypse, which relies on an understanding of the importance of history, did not infect traditional humans; they were as immune to worrying about or longing for the end times as they were incapable of it.

Beginning around 700 years BCE, however, in an era often referred to as the Axial Age, the stability and stasis of the traditional worldview began to erode. From the hills of Rome to the valleys of the Indus River to the dying wetlands of Mesopotamia, the entire placement of humanity in the universe was under question. This civilized world during the Axial Age was intricately connected—far more dynamic, globalized, and cosmopolitan than most of us remember from the dog-eared copies of our grade-school history books—a world that was churning with new ideas and influences and technologies and consumed by the ongoing struggles between great empires. By the middle of the first millennium BCE, trade had exploded across the civilized world, from the Indus valley to the Nile River and north to the Grecian peninsula and to the new city of Rome—trade not just in goods and materials but in ideas, rituals, and beliefs. Buddhist missionaries could be found in Athens, just as Egyptian traders frequented the streets of Bombay.[1] Ideas and philosophies were exchanged alongside silk, timber, and gold. It was during this time that the great philosophies and religions of Platonism, Buddhism, and Confucianism were first articulated, and that the seeds of Western thinking, from rationalism to monotheism, were sown. Like the trinkets that made their way on ancient trade caravans, these new ideas were borrowed, tried on, and discarded, and vestiges of the traditional worldview coexisted with the seminal ideas of the modern.

For most cultures during this period, the gods still lived in the mythical center of the circle, but increasingly, humankind began to conceive of the gods as beings who were deeply concerned with the new, unfolding history of man: the mythologies of the ancient Greeks and Romans are full of stories of the gods quarreling and taking sides in history. It was during this period that humanity's mythic gaze began to shift from the creative origins of the universe to its final destructive end; during this period that we began to imagine that instead of chaos and order as eternally balanced components of the universe, there were forces of good and evil destined for a final showdown. It was during this tumultuous age that people began to make the shift from a belief in circular time to linear time—although both would coexist in the Western mind until well beyond the Enlightenment. And it was during this period, in the efflorescent millennium before Christ, that some began to cultivate a belief in the imminent end of time, as well as the idea that when the end came, some would be saved and others would be damned. In short, many of the elements of our modern apocalypse—the strands of DNA and RNA of what would become our virus—could be found in many parts of the civilized world during the Axial Age. But these strands had yet to be brought together, and our incipient virus had yet to find a host.

At the crossroads of this newly civilized and interconnected world lay ancient Mesopotamia—the original melting pot, a place where cultures, languages, and systems of belief collided, merged, and disappeared or re-created themselves, often within the span of mere decades. And at the crossroads of Mesopotamia lay the Promised Land of Judea. At its most glorious height, Israel was at best a minor empire, perhaps not much more than a city-state—comprising less than one million people in a world of one hundred million humans at that time—that arose briefly between the tides of greater empires that were sweeping to and fro across the ancient Near East. Yet it is in Judea, and in the experiences of the Jewish people, that the disparate strands of apocalypse—a belief in a meaningful history, of a chosen people, and of an imminent overturning of the age—would come together and proceed to alter the course of history itself.

Despite a desire to see the equivalence of apocalyptic thought in other religions, there is no other way—not through Hinduism or Buddhism or Confucianism or any of the thousands of local beliefs mined today by New Age seekers—to arrive at our modern definition of the apocalypse than through the history of the Israelites. We don't believe in the apocalypse because ancient Mesoamericans had ideas about cycles of destruction and renewal or even because the Iranian prophet Zoroaster introduced many of the ideas that would form the template of the Judeo-Christian conception of apocalypse. The history of the apocalypse is the history of the Abrahamic traditions. The apocalypse is persistent in the modern Western world not because people have always been fixated on the end (they haven't) but because when the Jewish people articulated the idea of a final end of time and then began to anticipate it, they set the stage for the arrival of Jesus Christ. The history of Christianity would define the history of Europe; the history of Europe would define the history of America; and the history of America would define the modern world.

REINVENTING THE WORLD

When the Lord first spoke to him in the desert, Abraham was just your average, run-of-the-mill Mesopotamian polytheist. While wandering in the land of Canaan some four thousand years ago, Abraham made his initial covenant with God, a covenant that is typical of the Mesopotamian understanding of the relationship between humanity and the gods; this is the story of a man who chooses to worship one of the many Canaanite gods as a patron god in hopes that that patronage will reward him and his descendants. In the story of Abraham in the Old Testament, there is no mention, as yet, of the singularity or supremacy of the Israelites' god; indeed, it's not even clear in the earliest Israelite texts to which of the many Canaanite gods Abraham is speaking. (Many scholars have long argued that the anonymous "Lord" who appears to Abraham was the Canaanite god El; there are multiple other instances in the Old Testament in which the polytheistic Mesopotamian heritage of the early Israelites is evident, with the Lord appearing to take the name at various times of other Canaanite gods.[2] This early polytheistic strain would endure for several centuries in early Israelite history. Its late persistence is evident in the story of Moses chastising his fellow Israelites for worshipping the Golden Calf during the Exodus from Egypt, which is believed to have taken place nearly half a millennia after Abraham's original covenant with the Lord.[3])

Compare the god in the story of Abraham to the God in the final story in the Old Testament—the book of Daniel, the first apocalypse in the canon and the only one in the Old Testament—and one is struck by how radically different the cosmology is between the two. The first covenant between God and Abraham contains no mention of the singularity or supremacy of God—the Lord simply promises Abraham that if he adopts Him as his (patron) god, He will bless him and his descendants and bequeath to them a great nation.[4] The God in the book of Daniel, by comparison, is alone in the firmament. He controls all of history, down to the smallest fact: Daniel's fifth vision of the end of the world is so detailed that it represents the longest prophecy in the Bible.[5] The God in the book of Daniel has the power to reward those who have faith in him not merely with a homeland but, for the first time in Jewish scripture, with resurrection and an eternal bliss outside of historic time.[6] One could almost say that the two stories come from two different peoples: the first, the Israelites, who resemble traditional humans in their beliefs; the second, the apocalyptic Jews.

Comparing these two stories, which are so radically different in their worldviews, one must ask, how did they get there? Separated by little more than a millennium, what happened to the Israelites that caused them to invent a wholly new cosmology from Abraham—to radically rethink the role of God, humanity, and history and to embrace an apocalyptic eschatology?

The answer can be found not just in the tides of empire that swept over them, but in how the Israelites reacted to the centuries of defeat that they suffered at the hands of greater military powers.

If one looks at a map of the ancient world, one finds Israel and Judea between the great civilizations, between the Romans to the north and the Babylonians to the east and the Egyptians to the west. In the space of a few hundred years, after they had survived the Exodus in Egypt and wandered in the desert before finally arriving in the Promised Land to establish the Davidic Kingdom, the Israelites would be conquered nearly half a dozen times. The temple that they had built for Yahweh would be repeatedly desecrated and demolished. The static and essentially benign world of the ancients dissolved in the sweeping tides of empires and history, which buffeted the Israelites and cast them in exile from their long-promised kingdom. And an incredible series of events—their exile in Babylon, the influence of Persian priests, their subjugation at the hands of the Greeks—would fundamentally alter their view of the universe, God, and history. Their reaction to these events, wholly different from how others had reacted to similar situations before, would lead to the arrival of a different conclusion about the source of meaning in the universe. Meaning did not need to come from myth; rather, the Israelites discovered, meaning could be found in history. The Israelite reaction to the events that befell them in the millennium before Christ would lead inexorably toward the modern idea of apocalypse and would lay the foundation for a new religion that was explicitly apocalyptic—a religion whose success would transform the world and irrevocably shift humanity's mythic gaze from the origins of creation to the end of time.

In losing their place in the world, the Israelites would reinvent the meaning of the world.

EXILE IN BABYLON

By around 1000 BCE, the Israelites were at their zenith as an empire: David had united the twelve tribes of Israel, and the capital of Jerusalem had been founded in the hills of Judea. The promise God had made to Abraham had been fulfilled. David's son, Solomon, would build a proper temple for Yahweh after David's death, just as the Sumerian kings before him had built temples for their gods; in return, the Lord had promised David an enduring, hereditary monarchy over Israel: "Your throne shall be established forever."[7]

In fact, the throne would be brief. Internal dissent would soon tear apart the kingdom. Not long after Solomon's death, around 926 BCE, the ten tribes of the north revolted against the Davidic line, and the united houses split into the separate northern Kingdom of Israel and the southern Kingdom of Judah. As larger empires amassed power to the south and east of the Israelites, it was only a matter of time before external pressures would come to bear upon the divided Israelites. In 720 BCE, the northern Kingdom of Israel fell to the Assyrian Empire. A little more than a century later, in 597 BCE, the Babylonian king Nebuchadnezzar II laid siege to Jerusalem in the south.

Nebuchadnezzar's siege of Jerusalem would set in motion a series of events and ideas that would profoundly alter the Israelite cosmology—and humankind's relationship to history. When Jerusalem fell, the Babylonian forces looted the city, the palace, and the temple that Solomon had built, carrying off all the golden treasures that had decorated it for more than four hundred years. The Arc of the Covenant, which had held the Ten Commandments, became lost to history. Nebuchadnezzar rounded up the elite of Jerusalem—the remaining royal court and up to ten thousand craftsmen, government officials, and priests—and marched them seven hundred miles across the Syrian desert to Babylon, forcing them into exile from their promised land. Once in Babylon—living in the largest city in the world, a city resplendent with the wealth of empire—Israelite craftsmen were enlisted in the construction of the city's public works and monuments; educated elites were drafted into supportive roles in public administration and in the marketplace; and less-educated Israelites became house-hold servants and gardeners for the wealthiest Babylonians.[8] Those Hebrews left behind by Nebuchadnezzar's troops fled to Egypt and Syria, and from there traveled north into Europe, marking the beginning of the Jewish diaspora.

At this point, the Israelites, had they maintained the beliefs of other early Mesopotamian cultures, would likely have disappeared from history entirely. After all, the Israelites weren't the first people of the ancient Near East to suffer complete defeat and for-eign exile at the hands of an enemy. Nor were they the first to find themselves sent into exile in the capitals of more powerful empires. The stage had been set for the Israelites to simply assimilate into the Babylonian Empire, which at the time was consuming cultures and their patron gods with a voracious appetite. Assimilation had been the course that most peoples in the Near East had chosen when they found themselves swept up by the shifting tides of empire. "When a people experienced such overwhelming military defeats and such total political subjugation, the obvious conclu-sion was drawn: its patron deity was recognized as weaker than the patron deity of the conquerer. And once discredited, a god or god-dess was soon neglected and forgotten."[9] Your city was sacked by the Babylonians, and the temple to your god destroyed? Well, Marduk must have roughed up Yahweh in the mythical realm, the traditional Mesopotamian interpretation went. Time to worship the god of a new place and a new temple.

Some of the Israelites in Babylon, no doubt, chose this tradi-tional interpretation of events, believing that the Babylonian god Marduk was more powerful than Yahweh; indeed, once in Babylon and separated from their temple, numerous Israelites abandoned their faith in the god who had once promised them the land of

Canaan forever, only to let them lose it at the hands of Nebuchadnezzar. Yet other Israelites—those who had been moving toward a
more monotheistic interpretation of Yahweh—were not overly
impressed by Etemenanki, the towering ziggurat to the patron god
Marduk that loomed over the city where they would remain in
exile for more than fifty years. They were not ready to abandon
Yahweh, nor were they ready to believe that he had abandoned
them or had been defeated in the mythical realm. Instead, in
Babylon, in the slanting sun of the world's richest empire, the
former priests of Yahweh came upon an alternative and unprecedented interpretation to explain what had happened to them.

Having lost the promised land, the remaining Israelites dou-
bled-down on their bet on Yahweh. They concluded that they
were being punished by Yahweh for not worshipping him alone—
for being too tolerant of the polytheists who had lived among
them in Judea and who were even now abandoning Yahweh for the
Babylonian gods.[10] The faithful Israelites concluded that Yahweh
himself had sent the Babylonians to defeat them as a punishment
for their transgressions.

The Mesopotamian traditions had long held that the gods
might punish or abandon a people for transgressions. That was,
after all, the point of building the temples and ziggurats: to placate
the tempestuous gods. Yet unlike prior defeated peoples, the
Israelites in Babylon didn't conclude that Yahweh had voiced his
displeasure with them by abandoning them when the Babylonians
came. Nor did they interpret the destruction of the temple as a tangible manifestation of Marduk defeating Yahweh in the spiritual
realm. Instead, the Israelites believed that God himself had sent the
Babylonians to destroy the temple. That meant that Yahweh was so
omnipotent that he controlled not just the fate of the Israelites but

also the actions of even the most powerful kings and nations—even those kings and nations who worshipped other gods and who appeared to be conquering the Jews.[11] Despite their defeat, Yahweh was still in charge.

The implications of this new explanation were profound—marking a critical shift in focus from the present to a revelatory future and a radical development in our historic consciousness. For how could the Israelites simply dismiss history as profane, as traditional people had done, when the surging tides of history had almost completely erased nearly every element of their identity? They had lost the Promised Land, the temple, and the Arc of the Covenant. If the Israelites were to remain Israelites while separated from Jerusalem and their temple, if their fealty toward Yahweh were to remain intact, then the present moment had to become something more than a reflection of what was happening in the mythical realm of the Mesopotamian gods. Instead, the Israelites maintained, the defeat and persecution that they were suffering at the hands of the Babylonians in the here and now was simply further evidence that they would triumph in the end. They were a chosen people, and while history might be indecipherable to those who were caught up in its tempestuous tides, the Israelites concluded, history was no longer meaningless. Instead, God was an active conductor of history, and the events that happened in history could be understood as the very means through which God revealed his plans for humanity. For the first time, understanding history became central to understanding God's will and humankind's place in the cosmos.

From the depths of their suffering in Babylonian exile, the outlines of the central promise of apocalypse had emerged. Those who had maintained their faith in Yahweh would emerge from their

Babylonian captivity not as Israelites but as the Jewish people, fully conscious of themselves as historic beings and looking toward history for signs of God's plan for his chosen people.[12]

Yet the tides of history and empire were not yet done buffeting the Israelites, nor were all of the strands of the apocalypse yet assembled in the Jewish cosmology.

THUS SPOKE ZOROASTER

On a moonless October night in 539 BCE, when most of Babylon's inhabitants were either drunk or drunkenly asleep following a citywide festival honoring their patron god Marduk, the Persian army dammed up the Euphrates River upstream from Babylon, causing the Euphrates to drop to a depth of just two feet. In knee-deep water, the troops of Cyrus the Great—leader of the Achaemenid Persian Empire—marched up the channel through which the river had flowed beneath the city's impenetrable walls. They made their way into the center of Babylon with little resistance and proceeded to massacre many of the city's residents.[13]

In Babylon, the Hebrews had first begun to long for a leader who would restore the Kingdom of Judea and allow them to return to Jerusalem to rebuild the temple. Initially, this messiah was perceived not as a spiritual leader but as a political and military one.[14] Cyrus's arrival was seen by the Jews as the coming of that longed-for leader. According to Second Isaiah, God had decided that his people had suffered enough at the hands of the Babylonians, and so he anointed Cyrus as the messiah to come and free the Hebrews from Babylon. "I have called you by name and given you your title, though you have not known me,"[15] the patron god of a powerless people says of the most powerful man on earth, according to Second Isaiah. And because God had called the Persian leader, the Babylonian Empire had fallen, and the Jewish exile in Babylon had come to an end.

Cyrus freed the Jewish people and allowed them to return to Judea—even, it is said, providing funds from the imperial treasury to help them rebuild their temple at Jerusalem. Some of the Jews, having lived all their lives in Babylon, remained there to enjoy the religious freedoms that Cyrus has brought to his entire empire. Those who did return to Judea, however, experienced firsthand something that would become common in any apocalyptic promise: disappointment. The Hebrews who had been scattered to all the directions of the compass during the Babylonian diaspora half a century before did not all return to help rebuild the cities of the kingdom, as Isaiah had promised. And after decades of decay and neglect, Judea was an impoverished land. The fields were dry, and the trees did not applaud.[16]

Those Hebrews who returned to Judea were accompanied by Persian soldiers, who would establish and maintain military garrisons there for more than two centuries. And accompanying the Persian soldiers was a cadre of Zoroastrian priests, who brought with them a radically new vision of time and man's purpose in the universe, which would profoundly influence the Hebraic worldview.

Although Zoroastrianism today is largely confined to a few hundred thousand followers in India and in the mountains of Iran and Pakistan, nearly everyone in the Western world will be familiar with its central story—for it's largely our Abrahamic story, with different names. Many of its premises—a belief in linear time; in a dualistic worldview; in a final, climactic battle marking the end of history; and in a final judgment of the dead, all of which are foundational to apocalyptic thought—would eventually make their way into the Old and New Testaments and thus into the mythical archetypes of the Western mind.[17]

Zoroaster, who probably lived in the tenth century BCE, believed that in the beginning there had been only one god, a good and just god named Ahura Mazdā, who had created the world and everything in it. Ahura Mazdā represented truth and creation and all things good. Yet there was an equally powerful antagonist to Ahura Mazdā, called Angra Mainyu, who had chosen to side with evil and destruction—a figure those of us from the Judeo-Christian heritage would today recognize as the devil. Both Ahura Mazdā and Angra Mainyu had aides and allies in the world—prototypes of the angels and demons that to this day consume the Judeo-Christian imagination but that did not exist in the Hebraic tradition prior to Persian rule. These angels and demons, these forces of good and evil, Zoroaster believed, were engaged in an epic struggle for control over the world.[18]

According to Zoroaster's teachings, this struggle between good and evil was contained within a limited or bounded time, measured in thousand-year increments. When the final battle took place between good and evil, history and the physical world would come to an end. Furthermore, Zoroaster believed, that final battle would include the judgment of every human soul that had ever lived. Upon death, he preached, every individual's life would be judged, and good deeds and thoughts would be weighed against whatever evil that person had done. (Every individual's thoughts and actions were recorded in a Book of Life, which the Judeo-Christian tradition would also borrow from the library of Persian beliefs.) Death, under Zoroaster's teaching, became a court of moral judgment; and, according to Zoroaster's vision of the end, when the final battle came between good and evil, all the human beings who had ever lived would be resurrected for a final judgment. Those who had sided with Ahura Mazdā would live forever in a celestial paradise. Those who had sided with Angra Mainyu and his evil cohorts would be condemned forever. Through Zoroaster, the struggle between order and chaos in the mythical world became the battle between good and evil in history—and every human being had a role to play in that struggle.

Under Persian influence, the Jews came to see that they were more than the chosen people of a god who could act in history; they were embroiled in an epic fight between good and evil. Time itself was not just linear but purposeful—it led to the ultimate union with God, in an eternal bliss, separated from the trials of this world. The righteous, the good, the chosen—those who had faith and who had been faithful—would eventually triumph. They would be rewarded not with a Golden Age here on earth. When the final battle came, this world would not be renewed on the material plane. A different, divine world would arise—a radical departure from the Axial Age belief in cycles of material destruction and renewal.

For the Hebrews who had been freed from exile in Babylon, only to return to penury in Jerusalem, the idea that the ultimate reward would come not in this world but in the next one must have assuaged their historical disappointment. By the time Alexander the Great swept through Syria and Egypt on his way to conquering the Far East in the fourth century BCE, the Jewish expectation of political change in this world had evolved into an expectation of an otherworldly and climactic end to history. For the first time in the Judaic cosmology, the Promised Land was no longer literally about returning to Judea but about entering the Kingdom of God—a prerequisite concept for the arrival of Jesus.

After two centuries of Persian rule and influence, the Jewish people at last had all the elements of apocalypse in their cosmology. But even as they began to wait for the next world and an escape from history, history would become even more intolerable—and the ideas of good and evil, of the end of the age, would soon spark a revolt.

THE APOCALYPSE ARRIVES WITH ANTIOCHUS IV EPIPHANES

With all the strands of apocalyptic thought now in place within the Judaic view of the cosmos, the Hebrews would first articulate what we would today call an apocalyptic vision with the arrival of a particularly brutal Greek ruler—Antiochus IV Epiphanes.

Following the final defeat of the Persian Empire by Alexander the Great in the fourth century BCE, the Hebrews living in Judea lost the relative religious and cultural autonomy that they had enjoyed for nearly two centuries under the Persians. This was the third empire in just more than three centuries to have conquered Judea. With the Greeks came the process of Hellenization—the forced adoption of Greek customs and practices—which divided the Jewish people and threatened a precipitous loss of cultural identity.

This threat to the Jewish identity reached an apogee under the Greeks around 170 BCE, when the Seleucid Greek king, Antiochus IV Epiphanes, attacked Jerusalem and asserted his control over the Jewish people. Determined to force the Jews to abandon their religion and instead worship the Greek gods, Antiochus outlawed the practice of Jewish dietary laws, prayers to Yahweh, and observation of the Sabbath. Violation of the decrees was punishable by death. Women who had circumcised their infant sons were executed by Greek soldiers; their dead babies were hung around their necks to send a message that no one who continued to practice the customs of the Hebraic tradition would be spared.

Yet such atrocities simply inflamed a growing Jewish revolt, and in 167 BCE, Antiochus IV Epiphanes again attacked Jerusalem with his army and massacred thousands of the city's inhabitants. His forces occupied the temple and sacrificed a pig on its altar, then furthered the desecration by renaming it the Temple of Zeus and inviting prostitutes to take up residence within its sacred walls. In response to the brutality of Antiochus's persecution, a small band of Hebrews led by Judah Maccabee launched a guerilla war against Antiochus's forces and, three years later, in 164, regained the temple from the Greeks. (The reconsecration of the temple by the Maccabees is a moment still celebrated to this day as the feast of dedication, or Hanukkah.)

The cruelty of the Greeks inspired a flood of apocalyptic writing among the Jews, and it was around the time of the Maccabean Revolt and the most severe Greek oppression that the only apocalypse that would make its way into the Old Testament—the book of Daniel—was written. The book of Daniel was not about Greek oppression, at least not literally. Rather, like most apocalypses, the book of Daniel adopted the conceit of having been written much earlier to metaphorically explain current events. In the book of Daniel's case, its conceit was that it had been written nearly four hundred years earlier during the Babylonian Exile.[19]

The first half of the book tells such well-known stories as Daniel being thrown into the lion's den or his friends being thrown into a fiery furnace by an irate King Nebuchadnezzar, only to survive with nary a singe. Such stories likely provided courage and consolation to the Hebrews living under the cruel persecution of Antiochus IV Epiphanes. But it's in the second half of the book, when Daniel falls into a series of visions that are interpreted by the angel Gabriel, that the book of Daniel becomes recognizably apocalyptic. In his visions, Daniel sees that all the trials and tribulations that the Jews are facing—presumably, though not explicitly, at the hands of the Seleucid Greeks—are part of a larger struggle between a powerful "Ancient of Days" and the forces of evil. That struggle would soon culminate "at the time of the end" with the arrival of a powerful messiah—an idea that the Hebrews probably first encountered with the Zoroastrian priests.[20] This messiah would destroy the evil king who had desecrated the temple and would establish an everlasting kingdom for the righteous. The dead would be raised and judged, and those who had sided with righteousness would be rewarded with everlasting life.

The apocalyptic anticipation found in the book of Daniel—a belief that behind the trials of history and time lay a sense of meaning, a meaning that would soon be revealed to the righteous, who would be relieved of suffering—spread like wildfire. Although the Maccabees soon succeeded in their quest for independence from the Greeks, the Hebrews were riven by political and religious divisions and factions after two centuries of Hellenization. With so many internal disagreements, the apocalyptic anticipation became feverish—and widely diverse. Some sects wandered off into the desert to await the coming Kingdom of God. Others longed for a more worldly messiah, a king strong enough to bring the conflicting factions of the Hebrews together. Eventually the political and religious divisions after the brief interlude of the Maccabean kings brought the nation to the verge of civil war, and in 63 BCE, the Romans were invited into Jerusalem to help ensure stability—the fourth major empire to conquer the Hebrews in less than half a millennium. Judea became a protectorate of Rome; soon thereafter, Jewish self-governance came to end.

It was within this cauldron of internal dissension and apocalyptic anticipation that Jesus of Nazareth arrived to carry out his ministry.

THE FIRST VECTOR

With the arrival of the Romans in 63 BCE, Jewish culture had reached a nadir—while apocalyptic expectation was reaching new heights. No longer looking for the Promised Land or a return to the glorious days of the Davidic line, Hebraic expectation under Roman rule was for a total upending of the age—an escape from the terrors of history. Although it had taken more than five hundred years—from the exile in Babylon to subsequent Persian influence and the horrors of Hellenization—for Jewish eschatology to be affected by all of the strands of apocalyptic thought, once those elements were in place, humanity's mythic focus shifted from the world's beginnings to its end. Jesus could not have come any earlier, for the apocalypse was the context, the shared understanding through which he delivered his message of a new covenant with God. Had apocalyptic expectation not already been widespread in Judea and Palestine—without the expectation and longing among the Hebrews not just for a messiah but for a radical end to the age—Jesus's heralding that an otherworldly Kingdom of God was at hand would have made little sense to his contemporary listeners.

Like any great orator, however, Jesus understood the expectations and assumptions of his audience, and as a preacher he borrowed heavily from the emerging apocalyptic tradition. He promised the complete upheaval and end to the corrupt and venal age—an upheaval that many had been eagerly anticipating for more than a century and a half. Echoing Daniel and other apocalyptic prophets before him, Jesus preached that the temple would be destroyed, with every stone thrown down to prepare the way for the building of God's new kingdom on earth, and that the arrival of that kingdom would coincide with the Day of Judgment, the raising of the dead, and the granting of eternal salvation to the blessed.[21] With incredible skill, Jesus of Nazareth wove together all the past threads of Jewish apocalyptic expectation into a compelling and strikingly contemporaneous narrative.

But perhaps most importantly, the words, life, and death of Jesus brought a renewed sense of urgency—a sense of imminence—to apocalyptic expectation. On the night of his arrest, in the so-called Olivet discourse (or "Little Apocalypse") contained within the synoptic Gospels of Matthew, Mark, and Luke, Jesus laid out his most specific description of what the end times would look like. Again echoing the apocalyptic prophecy of Daniel, Jesus declared that at the end of time there would be wars and rumors of wars, false prophets, earthquakes, and famines.[22] Yet as to the specific timing of these events, Jesus provides two seemingly contradictory messages. The first was that no one except God knows the hour and the day when the end will come. But it is his second answer—that "this generation will not pass away till all these things take place"[23]—that marked Jesus's great contribution to the rhetoric of apocalypse.

This renewed sense of imminence signified a massive change in how people thought about the end of the world, which for nearly all human history had been imagined (if it had been imagined at all) as taking place in some impossibly distant or mythical time. This immediacy of expectation served as the first (and arguably most important) vector of our virus, providing relevance and resonance to the rapidly growing Jewish cult of Christ. The apocalypse was no longer merely the promise of a better world or of a messiah yet to come in some distant, prophesied future. The better world was here, the Messiah had come, and he might return to complete his work and judge all humanity at any second.[24] Certainly, the end of the world could come within our lifetimes, the early Christians thought, contradicting Ecclesiastes's famous axiom. This *was* something new under the sun: the first explicitly apocalyptic religion the world had ever seen, a faith whose central tenet was the anticipation of the imminent second coming of Christ—and the imminent end of history.

Yet Jesus's contradictory explanations presented a problem to the earliest Christians in the years after his death. Those who lived contemporaneously with Jesus fervently believed his declaration that "this generation will not pass away till all these things take place." Indeed, most early Christians believed that they were *already* living at the end of time, a belief that many Christians maintain to this day. To the first generation of Christians, Jesus was seen as the first of all the dead to be resurrected; his resurrection represented the beginning of the universal judgment, and his return, they believed, was imminent.[25] The earliest letters of Saint Paul to the Corinthians, written around 50 CE, present to us a window through which we can view the earnestness of this expectation. In his letters, Paul urges the faithful to stay true to Christ's teachings: don't be distracted by worldly concerns, he advises them; don't even bother marrying, he says, for "the appointed time has grown very short."[26] Like the author of the book of Daniel before him, Paul saw the proper role of the apocalyptic believer as one of not acting to change the world (as the Maccabees had done) but one of remaining true to one's principles while awaiting the transformation of the world by God.

But if the end of the age is imminent, why isn't it already here? Why hasn't it come? It would soon prove untenable for the believers in Christ to exist in the world without participating in it—to simply wait for the return of Jesus, as Paul had earlier urged the Corinthians. After all, constantly waiting for the end of the world is exhausting—and disappointing, as the earliest Christians learned. The generation of believers who had known Jesus in the flesh began to pass away, and still Christ had not come back again. Hope for his return was rekindled in 66 CE, when the Jewish people finally revolted against the Roman occupation; the Christians expected that triumph for the Jews would also herald the return of Christ to establish his kingdom on earth. But things turned out very differently: in 70 CE, the Romans laid brutal siege to Jerusalem, and once again the temple was destroyed. Yet even with the temple's destruction, Christ did not return.[27]

So what had Jesus meant? He had clearly preached that the end of the historical age and the arrival of the Kingdom of God was at hand; but decades later, history still marched on, the eon had not ended, and the lot of the Jews and the early Christians was as miserable as it had ever been. A new understanding of Jesus's apocalyptic message was required. When Roman persecution of the Christians increased following the failed Jewish revolt, the book of Revelation—essentially a Christian recasting of the book of Daniel, a fantasy of destruction followed by a coda of powerless and despondent longing—was written to provide for suffering believers the assurance of the Lord's imminent return.[28] The growing urgency and desperation for that return can be heard in Revelation's final, famously imploring sentence: "Come, Lord Jesus."[29]

Seventy years after the death of Jesus, a major problem with his apocalyptic promise had been revealed. How could believers in Christ live in history, in an age that clearly was not ending? When would the Kingdom of God arrive? Date setting came into vogue, and Christians looked for the promised signs of Christ's return everywhere. But dates came and went, and the signs that seemed certain signified nothing. How could Christianity deal with the problem of an imminent apocalypse that was forever delayed?

One solution can be found in the Gospel of Saint John, which was written around 100 CE, a few decades after the earlier synoptic Gospels of Matthew, Mark, and Luke had been put down. John's solution to the problem of an imminent—yet forever delayed—apocalypse was strikingly simple: he redacted, nearly entirely, Jesus's apocalyptic preachings. In the Gospel of Saint John, Jesus is presented as more of a symbolic than a historic figure. John emphasizes that Jesus himself is "the way, the truth, and the life";[30] faith in him alone will grant one salvation, regardless of when (or even if) the end of time comes. The Gospel of Saint John eliminates the Olivet discourse—the prophesy of the end times that Jesus delivered to his disciples on the night before his arrest in the earlier synoptic Gospels. The Kingdom of God—so central to Jesus's message in the earlier tellings of his life—is mentioned a mere two times, and when it is mentioned, it is conceived through a dialectic that renders moot the question of when the kingdom will come: the kingdom is at once "already now" and "not yet."[31] According to John, the believer in Christ has already been judged, so why would it matter when the final judgment day comes?[32] A

Christian doesn't have to look anymore for Jesus to return in history, the Gospel of Saint John argues, for although the Christian still lives in the world, he or she, like Christ himself, is no longer *of* the world.[33]

Yet despite John's best efforts, it would prove difficult, if not impossible, to fully divorce the life and teachings of Jesus—arguably the greatest apocalyptic preacher in history—from the apocalypse itself. Understanding what he meant, and interpreting the problem of apocalypse that he had left behind, would become a central question of Christian theology. Over time, each new interpretation would be like an adaptation in the evolution of the apocalypse—broadening its appeal and allowing it to spread to ever-larger populations.

But for the moment, the apocalypse remained contained largely in the Sinai, among the small sect of Hebrews who believed in Christ's apocalyptic message. Before it could become a powerful new religion that would spread across and transform the world, the apocalypse would require a new vector.

APOCALYPSE WHEN?

That new vector came with the decline of the Roman Empire. As the empire began its slow unraveling, and as the economic security once provided to many of the citizens of the Roman Empire began to dissipate, the appeal of Christianity—with its apocalyptic promise of revolutionary change to the downtrodden—grew in strength and reach. This rapid spread of Christianity among the populace further weakened the empire's tenuous stability, until the year 312 CE, when Constantine I adopted Christianity as the religion of the Roman Empire following his victory at the Battle of the Milvian Bridge. If the apocalyptic and anti-imperial expectations of the fast-growing religion threatened the empire, Constantine concluded, then the safest course was to make the apocalyptic expectations of the populace *part* of the empire. After all, the populace's expectation of later rewards had its merits.

That there was a certain irony to this hardly mattered to our virus. A virus doesn't care about irony; it cares about spreading and surviving. Ideas that had been cultivated in defiance of empire would now have to be revised to sustain empire. The fundamentally revolutionary message of Jesus's apocalyptic preachings, with their condemnation of the powerful, would have to be squared with an increasingly politically powerful church. The apocalypse could not be separated from the Christian faith. Instead, what Christ had meant when he said that the Kingdom of God was at hand would have to be revised.

The adoption of Christianity by Constantine sparked a new interest in using the rhetoric of apocalypse to solidify political power, with Eusebius of Caesarea espousing a new, imperial eschatology to replace the revolutionary expectation of Jesus's message. Eusebius cultivated the idea that God had chosen the Roman Empire to spread Christianity throughout the world. What Jesus had been referring to when he referred to the Kingdom of God was not revolutionary change but the Roman Empire itself; the Roman emperors had succeeded Christ, Eusebius maintained, in order to fulfill God's divine plan on earth. At the end of history (which was a very long time off, Eusebius assured a nervous Constantine on his throne), Christ would return to succeed the Roman emperors.

But Christ did not return to supplant the emperors as the Roman Empire continued its collapse over the next century.

Instead, the Church soon found itself in ascendant power over the human-made world, while in the pews the revolutionary rumblings of Jesus's apocalypse continued to gain strength. With the acceptance of the Revelation of Saint John into the canon, an increasing number of lay millennialists—those who believed that Christ would physically return to reign over the earth for a thousand years—tried to deduce, through interpretations of the book of Revelation, the exact date of his return. This rise in millennialist expectation threatened the Church's attempt to fill the political vacuum left by the empire's collapse, as those awaiting Christ's return and an imminent end tended to be unruly. For the second time in a century, those in power found themselves with the need to revise the meaning and intent of Jesus's apocalyptic message.

That second revision was provided, quite eloquently, by Augustine of Hippo in his masterful work *The City of God*, written between 413 and 426. Unlike Eusebius, who had tried with only a modicum of success to shoehorn the Christian expectation of apocalypse into the political order of his day, Augustine proposed that Jesus's preaching of an apocalyptic end to the current age was always meant to be allegorical rather than literal. Simply by believing in Christ, according to Augustine, one was *already* dwelling in the Kingdom of God; the timing of the Last Judgment and the Parousia (the Second Coming) was therefore of little relevance to one's faith. The people, Augustine argued, should stop concerning themselves with the end of time and become focused instead on the divine that was already present in the material world, represented in the form of the Catholic Church.[34] Augustine's work, as historian and educator Paul Boyer has pointed out, "distanced Catholic thought from all literalist readings of prophecy, and especially from notions of an earthly millennialism."[35] With apocalyptic anticipation effectively condemned as a foolish waste of time, Saint Augustine attempted to push the anticipation of the end of the world out of the mainstream of the Christian faith. After Augustine, the offhand dismissal of those who believed in the imminent end of the world became the requisite pose of the intellectual, political, and religious elite.

Yet Augustine's metaphorical interpretation created unexpected consequences. At the time that Augustine was so eloquently dissuading the faithful from too closely interpreting the apocalypse within history, more of the faithful were exposed to the book of Revelation through its newfound acceptance into the canon. Augustine "made the apocalyptic part of the everyday fabric of Christian life and belief, and . . . reinforced eschatological awareness by embedding it in liturgy and preaching."[36] By the time Augustine was finished with his argument that the apocalypse was a metaphor, even those who weren't inclined to want a radical end of the age found themselves thinking apocalyptically. The apocalypse had mutated from a literal expectation of radical change, which could be rejected on any number of grounds, to an expectation of metaphorical change, which could be accepted for personal reasons. By explicitly becoming metaphor, the apocalypse was able to deepen its influence for nearly a thousand years, appealing to a much wider population.

Despite Augustine's best efforts, by the early fifth century, apocalyptic anticipation, with its promise of an upheaval of the current order, was again sweeping the Christian world, and date setting was as popular as ever. This millennialist fervor threatened the Church's ability to maintain order. As Paul had articulated in those early dusty days when the first Christians had awaited the return of Christ, the problem with believing that the end is imminent is that one's current obligations seem rather pointless. Why bother milking the cows when the end is nigh?

The Church's solution to the threatening laziness and "dangerous speculations" of the commoners was one that we would recognize in how our own politicians deal with the intractable problems looming in the near future: they kicked the can farther down the road.[37] In the early fifth century, Christian historians such as Orosius and Victorious of Aquitane hastily recalculated the age of the earth, determined that Christ had actually come in the year 5200, and declared that the end of the world (sorry to disappoint!) was actually three hundred years away.[38] The message of Orosius and Victorious was clear: get back to work, because nothing is changing. Not by coincidence, it would be almost precisely 225 years later—in 725 CE, as the end of the world (according to the official calculations of Orosius and Victorious) again approached —that the English monk Bede the Venerable would pen *On the Reckoning of Time* and adopt an idea originally proposed by Dionysius Exiguus two centuries before: the division of the world not into six ages of 1,000 years each, beginning with creation, but into two ages, demarked by the Incarnation—what we now refer to as BC (Before Christ) and AD (Anno Domini, the Year of Our Lord).[39] This new calendar "was open-ended and without apocalyptic implications," as religious scholar Stephen O'Leary has put it.[40] Originally dismissed as a heretic, Bede would become one of the most influential figures of the Middle Ages, in no small part because, through his work, the expectation of the end of the world could be delayed indefinitely—a trick of apocalyptic suspension that those who ruled the world had tried to master for more than seven hundred years.

Among the people, apocalyptic anticipation would quietly

maintain its hold over the popular imagination of Europe for the next thousand years. Like a virus, apocalyptic belief spread throughout Europe with the spread of Christianity, but it went through alternating periods of latency and virulence, flaring up here and there at different times and in different regions, only to then die down again, awaiting the return of the right vector.[41]

The virus went through a brief but important evolution in the twelfth century, when the Italian monk Joachim of Fiore rejected Augustine's interpretation of the apocalypse as simply an allegory for the fate of the human soul and "vigorously reintroduced millenarianism."[42] He calculated (from his readings of Revelation) that the end of the current age would take place in 1260, following a terrible conflict between two rival popes, one of whom was the Antichrist; following this battle, the Catholic Church would be ruled by a new order of just and benevolent monks. Most importantly, however, Joachim preached that human actions could help usher in the final Age of the Spirit—a new mutation of our virus of apocalyptic thinking that would soon prove lethal.

A PANDEMIC IN EUROPE

During the fourteenth and fifteenth centuries, the thousand-year attempt by the Catholic Church to keep the revolutionary nature of the apocalypse at bay finally began to falter. The papal tradition of collecting indulgences—a sort of tax on sins—was increasingly viewed as rapacious by the masses, who grew restive under the control of a Church that, more and more, was seen as corrupt. As the countryside of Europe was swept first by the Black Death and then by the marauding armies of the Hundred Years' War, conditions were ripe for a resurgence of apocalyptic preachings of deliverance from this miserable world. For the beleaguered peasants of late Middle Age Europe, whether that deliverance was political or spiritual hardly mattered anymore.

This was an age of tremendous turmoil—a level of turmoil the likes of which the Christian faith had not seen since the collapse of the Roman Empire. In 1378, the death of Pope Gregory XI (who was viewed by much of Europe as being excessively pro-French and irredeemably corrupt) threw the Catholic Church into chaos. In what became known as the Western Schism, two separate men emerged to declare themselves Gregory's successor as pope and emperor of the Holy Roman Empire. In 1415, bishops and leaders of the Catholic Church came together at the Council of Constance to resolve the crisis, but when they voted to execute one of the new pope's principal opponents and a leading advocate of Church reform—Jan Hus of Prague—an open revolt erupted in the hills of Bohemia.[43]

That revolt marked the beginning of centuries of bloodshed in Europe that was inflamed by explicitly apocalyptic rhetoric. Our virus of apocalypse had finally evolved into a pandemic: for the first time in European history, apocalyptic warfare broke out, with fighters on both sides believing that their battles would bring about the end of time. The Taborites, as the rebellious followers of Jan Hus in Bohemia came to be known, believed that the new millennium had already arrived with the ascendancy of the new pope, whom they denounced as the Antichrist. The final days were at hand, the Taborites believed. Echoing Joachim's belief that human agency could help usher in the return of Christ, the Taborites set out to cleanse the world of sin and to prepare the way for Christ's arrival by killing heretics—a duty they fulfilled through multiple massacres of those loyal to Rome.[44] Recruiting local peasants with promises that the order of the world was soon to be overturned, the Taborites armed the peasants of Bohemia with hand cannons (the first widespread use of gunpowder weapons in European warfare) and fought the papal armies to a near standstill for more than fifteen years.

The Taborites' apocalyptic rhetoric was soon able to spread even more rapidly, thanks to a revolutionary new technology. The invention of the Gutenberg printing press began to put the Bible—and, more importantly, the book of Revelation—into the hands of hundreds of thousands of Europeans in the decade following the end of the Taborite rebellion. Perhaps the Church could have withstood popular discontent with its corrupt practice of collecting indulgences; perhaps it could have continued to overcome the armed rebellion of groups like the Taborites; but it could not withstand the new technology of the printing press, which steadily gave a newly literate populace the ability to draw its own conclusions about the meaning of the Bible's most fascinating and oblique book. A thousand years after Augustine, his work was being undone by the ability of those in the pews to ignore the metaphorical preachings coming from the pulpit. Thanks to rising literacy rates, the European masses by the end of the fifteenth century had become intimately familiar with the book of Revelation —and thus were primed for a political narrative framed around the end of an age.

By the time Martin Luther nailed his *Ninety-Five Theses* to the door of the All Saints' Church in 1517, familiarity with the apocalyptic metaphor among the European masses was at a zenith— and it was a familiarity that Luther was more than willing to exploit in service to his cause. Although he himself subscribed to

Augustine's view that the Kingdom of God was an allegorical, rather than a historical, truth, and though he doubted the canonicity of Revelation, Luther readily labeled Pope Leo X to be the Antichrist.[45] To foment popular support for his demands, Luther declared that "we have no more temporal things to expect," for the Kingdom of God on earth was at hand.[46] Again.

But Luther soon realized that the power of the apocalyptic promise, once unleashed on a populace newly empowered through literacy and the spread of books, was impossible to contain. Luther was dismayed by the rise of the radical Anabaptists out of the Reformation movement, whose millennialist preachings contributed to the largest popular uprising in Europe prior to the French Revolution—the bloody Peasants' Wars of 1524–1525, in which more than one hundred thousand people were slaughtered.[47]

The Anabaptists' militant apocalypticism reached its height when they took control of the city of Münster in the mid-1530s, declared the city the "New Jerusalem," and exiled all those who didn't believe the end was nigh. Instead of God's kingdom on earth, however, Münster was hell on earth: its leaders instituted Old Testament law, mandated polygamous marriage, and burned every book in the city that wasn't the Bible. After a long siege, the royal army took the city back and massacred the Anabaptists. Their self-appointed king—who had "declared that he would rule as king of the world until Jesus personally came to take David's scepter from his hand"[48]—was captured and, along with two other leaders of the rebellion, brutally tortured to death. Their bodies were thrown into cages and hung from the steeple of Saint Lambert's Church, where they remained for fifty years as a warning to those who would engage in apocalyptic rebellion. (The cages remain hanging from the steeple to this day.)

The pandemic was over. After Münster and the Protestant Reformation, the apocalyptic virus would largely fade from mainland Europe. In part this was because the impetus for the outbreak of apocalyptic fever in the late Middle Ages—discontent with papal influence over nationalist affairs and disgust with the corrupt and increasingly regressive collection of indulgences—was removed with the advent of Lutheran and other Protestant churches. It may not have been God's kingdom on earth, but at least it wasn't the pope's. With the political crisis resolved and behind them, many Protestant thinkers and clergy abandoned the apocalyptic rhetoric that had so effectively recruited the masses to their cause. The new Protestant churches largely returned to the amillennialism of Augustine, which had so well served Catholic leaders before them in suppressing the revolutionary nature of apocalyptic belief among the pews. Apocalyptic rhetoric would make later appearances—in the dialectic of Karl Marx in the nineteenth century and in the rhetoric of the Nazis in the twentieth—but with the beginning of the seventeenth century and the Age of Enlightenment, the apocalyptic virus would never again prove as influential in continental Europe, which was well on its way to becoming the largely secularized continent that we know today.

In England, however, where the Anglican Church tried to strike a balance between Catholicism and Protestantism, the apocalyptic still had a major role to play in driving historical and political change. It would take another century, through the English Civil Wars and Oliver Cromwell and the Glorious Revolution and the Fifth Monarchists, before the power of the apocalyptic would begin to dissipate in England.

How far our little virus had traveled: from its early evolution in the Sinai and the beginnings of humankind's historical consciousness, the apocalypse had spread northward with the Holy Roman Empire, transforming the map of Europe and man's view of his place in the cosmos; it had become a constant companion to the unfolding story of Western civilization. Yet the bloodshed in continental Europe that followed the Reformation and the new political order in England had largely inoculated the population of Europe to promises of a radical end to the age. What our virus needed was a new vector—and a new population to infect. And as luck would have it, it would find a whole new continent, a continent whose history would change the course of the world in the coming centuries. The Puritans, who rejected the Anglican compromise between Catholicism and Protestantism, would soon set out from Southampton to begin a new nation—the first nation in the history of the world founded on explicitly apocalyptic principles.

The apocalypse had arrived in America.

CHAPTER 4

THE RAPTURE
OF AMERICA

It's little wonder that we think the idea of the apocalypse has always been a part of the human condition, for in America, the apocalypse has never been far from the center of everyday life. Sit down at your breakfast table on any given morning, and the coming Kingdom of God is at equal arm's length as the butter or jam. The Shaker table and ladder-back chair you may sit at were built with simplicity in preparation for the coming return of Christ. The Oneida® silverware you reach for is the capitalist remnant of a millennialist cult.[1] Pass the cornflakes, and you inadvertently serve up the end of the world: John Kellogg, a Seventh-Day Adventist, invented the breakfast cereal to develop millennial perfection for the body. (His brother William, more concerned with riches in this world than with rewards in the next, soon added sugar to the recipe, building a global food empire on the sweetened result.)[2]

The influence of the apocalypse on American history extends far beyond a survey of the breakfast table. On his return journeys to America, Christopher Columbus, delirious from syphilis, believed he would rediscover the Garden of Eden on the new continent, thus fulfilling a necessary prerequisite (as was believed at the time) for the return of Christ. Columbus's vision of America as the New Israel was shared by the Puritans. Puritan lawyer John Winthrop's oft-cited description of America as "a city upon a hill,"[3] invoked in his sermon from the decks of the *Arbella* before the colonists had even made landfall on the new continent, imagined America shining as a beacon of millennial preparation and spiritual cleanliness. It was not, as the phrase would later be reinterpreted by President Ronald Reagan (and by President John F. Kennedy before him), shining as a lighthouse of democratic example. And the first American bestseller, owned at one time by one out of every twenty citizens in the Bay Colony, was *The Day of Doom*—a 1662 poem by the clergyman Michael Wigglesworth that delighted Puritan households with its graphic tales of sinners being cast into hell on Judgment Day.[4]

This obsession with the apocalypse in America is not confined to the distant past. Today, more than 40 percent of Americans believe that Christ will return within their lifetimes. An equal number believe that the Bible should be taken literally as the actual Word of God. (As a point of comparison, in Great Britain, where religious apocalypticism made its last stand in Europe some three and a half centuries ago, a mere 6 percent of adults believe the Bible is literally inerrant.) And while those with more secular beliefs may like to dismiss the apocalyptic as being the exclusive domain of the religious, still another 30 percent of Americans today believe that an asteroid will strike the Earth in the next forty years, while 58 percent believe the next few decades will see a new world war.[5]

Yet apocalyptic anticipation wasn't the only intellectual stowaway from Europe that arrived with the earliest settlers of America. For other colonists, there was a competing ideal that sought to give meaning and purpose not just to the founding of the new nation but to history itself—the ideal of progress. Indeed, if America is exceptional in one indisputable way, it is that America is the only nation to be founded on *both* the competing ideals of apocalypse and progress. This bifurcated founding is what makes us at once idealistic—known the world over for our friendliness and optimism—and fatalistic—possessed more strongly than many nations by the sense that doom lies just around the corner. In addition, this bifurcated founding allows us to be at once the exemplar of republican democracy and the most religious of all the modern nations.

Where did our faith in progress come from? In the aftermath of the bloodshed that had followed the Reformation, European intellectuals were left with an understandable distaste for a worldview that longed for a cataclysmic end to an age that would provide meaning to the vagaries of history. They had seen that social upheaval and human-made apocalyptic mayhem had not prepared the way for the return of Christ, as Joachim of Fiore and the radical Anabaptists had argued. But was the role of humankind to do nothing, to simply wait, as the opponents of the Maccabees and then Paul himself had argued, for the arrival of the perfect age? Or was there yet another alternative, another purpose for humanity in history?

To answer that question, the European intelligentsia looked back to the days of Plato and Aristotle and revived the Greek belief in the material progress of humankind through history.[6] While most cultures of late antiquity still held the traditional notion of the Declining Ages of Man, by the fifth century BCE, a countercurrent in ancient Greek thought began to imagine that the Greek age and civilization were *better* than what had come before—and that things were improving. As evidenced from the pronouncements of Plato's Protagoras in *The Laws* and beyond, the Greeks began to believe that a new Golden Age was achievable through the pursuit of education, justice, and virtue.[7]

Borrowing heavily from such classical sources, Europeans following the Reformation came to understand that man could
improve his own lot through reason and industry. Through the
advancement of scientific knowledge, and the discovery of the laws
of nature, these early Enlightenment thinkers believed that man
could come to understand God in the material world and that
through his own hard work and the steady, progressive accumulation of knowledge and wisdom, man himself could create the
Kingdom of God on earth. This was not a sudden turn toward secularism—but it was a critical juncture in the journey toward it. For
early rationalist thinkers like Francis Bacon and René Descartes,
the objective of rationalism and science was not to disprove the
existence of God but to show that God existed through empirical
observation. As Galileo is often said to have commented early in
the seventeenth century, "Mathematics is the language with which
God has written the universe"—hardly the declaration of a scientist bent on disproving God's existence.[8]

Over time, however, each discovery of the new, empirical science that emerged from rationalist thinking further undermined
the traditional Christian view of an interventionist God. Discoveries such as Newton's laws of motion in the seventeenth century
and the Linnaean classification of species in the eighteenth century
led many to further reconsider, and even doubt, God's relationship
to the world.[9] During the nineteenth century, discoveries in the
new science of geology revealed that the world was far older than
the six thousand years that biblical scholars had previously
assumed. Darwin's theory of evolution, though widely misunder-
stood and frequently misapplied in the social sphere, soon led
many to believe that humans were the pinnacle and triumph of the
world, the perfect form that nature had spent millions of years

trying to attain. Within just three centuries of the Reformation, the Judeo-Christian story of the world's creation had been supplanted by a new, secular, and scientific explanation in the minds of millions of people around the world. By the end of the nineteenth century, Nietzsche, surveying the upending of the Christian worldview by science and empiricism, would borrow a phrase from Hegel and declare, "God is dead," adding, most importantly, "And we have killed him."[10]

Yet if God was dead from history, how could humankind find meaning in history? Traditional people had viewed history as meaningless; the Judeo-Christian tradition viewed history as the stage upon which God unveiled his plan for humankind, which would end in apocalypse; but for the secular mind, history become the place where man, not God, would fulfill his potential and become the master of the world. In place of God's plan, humanity's achievements would give history its purpose.

The Enlightenment ideal of progress, in short, became the modern antidote for the apocalyptic virus that had plagued the Western mind for nearly two thousand years. The discoveries of universal laws that guided the functions of the universe had led men like Voltaire and Rousseau—and, in America, Thomas Jefferson and the other Founders—to begin to imagine that there were universal rights and laws that should guide humankind. Social upheaval, and the rhetoric behind it, began to be powered not simply by religious discontent but by a secular desire for social and economic betterment—by the idea of progress. By the time of the American Revolution, new discoveries in science and new principles of self-governance and the inherent rights of man had succeeded in replacing God as the conductor of history. Perfection could be achieved without an apocalyptic cataclysm; perfection could be achieved through progress. Man, not God, would conduct the symphony.

From the beginning, this combination of our faith in progress and our belief in apocalypse has conspired to create a uniquely American understanding of the world and our place within it. The idea of humankind's material progress through history, rediscovered by European thinkers during the Enlightenment, greatly influenced the Calvinist ethic of hard work and industry among America's earliest religious settlers. The idea of progress was also deeply intertwined with apocalyptic anticipation in the Puritan mind; even as early New England preachers such as Increase Mather and Cotton Mather preached the end of the world, they advocated lifelong education, believing that the study of classical works should begin at a young age and continue throughout one's life so that one could continuously better oneself. Later, as revolutionary fervor swept the colonies, the rhetoric of the American Revolution proclaimed a secular and civic responsibility to spread the cause of liberty throughout the earth—echoing the earliest European settlers of America, who believed the sacred duty of Americans was to spread Christianity through prayer, morality, and mission. Throughout the course of the Revolution, rhetoricians declared King George III to be the Antichrist and promised that the spread of the Gospel and republican principals of freedom would bring about the Millennium.[11] By the middle of the nineteenth century, the synthesis between progress and apocalyptic purpose would become apparent in the belief that America had a Manifest Destiny to expand across the continent and, later, during the twentieth century, to spread and defend democracy throughout the world. This melding of apocalyptic destiny with the promise of progress and democracy has created the American worldview. As Herman Melville put it: "We Americans are the peculiar, chosen people—the Israel of our time; we bear the ark of liberties of the world."[12]

Yet if progress and apocalypse in America have at times cross-fertilized each other, at other times progress and apocalypse have been at poisonous odds with each other. The religious movements that defined much of American history during the nineteenth century represented a long-running argument between the religious American mind and the steadily encroaching victories of technological, scientific, and industrial progress. And while it's probably coincidental, it's certainly emblematic that the year the word *scientist* was first coined—1833—was the same year the Baptist preacher William Miller announced that his studies of biblical prophecy had revealed that the return of Christ was imminent within the decade.[13]

Miller was among the first to revive the doctrine of *premillennialism*—the notion that Christ will physically return to earth prior to the thousand-year reign promised in chapter 20 of the book of Revelation. Christ's return, premillennialists believe, will signify the beginning of the Tribulations, a period during which believers will be separated from nonbelievers, the latter of whom will suffer unspeakable horrors before the final Judgment Day and the end of history.

The reintroduction of premillennialism during the early nineteenth century represented a radical shift in apocalyptic belief. For nearly fourteen hundred years—ever since Saint Augustine constructed his *amillennial* argument that the thousand-year reign of Christ was meant to be understood metaphorically rather than literally—premillennialism had largely disappeared from mainstream Christian thought. Those who rejected amillennialism were *postmillennialists*, who believed that the return of Christ would happen only *after* the Church had achieved God's kingdom on earth.[14] Postmillennial rhetoric was employed during the Protestant Reformation to whip European peasants into battle on the promise that their victory would pave the way for the return of Christ; less violently, the Puritans married their postmillennialist beliefs to the emerging ideal of progress, believing that their industry and steadfastness would make America into the shining city on the hill that would be admired by the entire world—and that would create the New Israel over which Jesus would rule.

For the American premillennialist movement that swept the country in the 1840s, however, the shining city on the hill was irrelevant. All human progress was folly, and the end times were at hand. The "Great Disappointment" that fell upon the more than 50,000 Millerites who awaited the end of the world in 1844 hardly dampened religious America's growing enthusiasm for this new, radical return to premillennialism. The Shakers and the Oneida community believed that the millennial kingdom had been initiated through their groups and practices; the Latter-Day Saints moved west to found the New Zion and await Christ's return; and the Jehovah's Witnesses declared, a generation after the memory of the Great Disappointment had faded, that the Second Coming of Christ had in fact already occurred in 1874.

The acrimonious relationship between progress and apocalypse, first expressed in the flourishing of premillennial experimentation that took place in America during the early nineteenth century, would eventually morph into a new and largely American strain of the virus of old Europe. But we weren't quite there with the Millerites, or the Mormons, or the Jehovah's Witnesses. It would take the ideas of a relentlessly self-promoting Irishman, a jail cell conversion, and one of the first blockbuster bestsellers in America before the apocalypse would mutate into the nearly ubiquitous strain that we know today: the Rapture.

THE DISPENSATIONS OF CYRUS SCOFIELD

Cyrus Scofield was a drunk, a liar, and a thief—which is a nice way of saying he was a politician from Kansas. A two-time state senator who became the youngest US District Attorney in the country at the age of twenty-nine, his career in politics was marred by accusations of bribery, corruption, and forgery. He resigned his DA position when it became known that he had perjured himself regarding his service in the Confederate Army. In 1879, this "peer among scalawags"[15] (as his hometown paper described him at the time) found himself sitting without bail in a St. Louis jail cell, accused of swindling his mother-in-law of her last $1,800 by selling her land that did not exist.[16]

And it was in this St. Louis jail cell where the seeds of the notion that Christ would soon Rapture up his faithful found the fertile soil of America.

Although it's impossible to place the precise moment of Scofield's conversion to Christianity (throughout his life, Scofield told many different versions of where and when he had found Christ), at least one version of his conversion takes place in that jail cell. Mending his ways, he was soon released and, despite having no theological training or background, immediately found himself under the influence and tutelage of a St. Louis Presbyterian minister, James Brookes. Brookes, in turn, had been one of the organizers of the Niagara Bible Conference of 1875, and he had returned to St. Louis to spread the latest brand of apocalyptic understanding among evangelicals—the dispensationalist teachings of an Irish preacher by the name of John Nelson Darby.

For nearly 1,700 years, Christian theologians had interpreted Paul's description of the return of Christ in his first letter to the Thessalonians in 52 CE ("and the dead in Christ shall rise first: Then we which are alive and remain shall be caught up together with them in the clouds, to meet the Lord in the air"[17]) primarily as metaphor. In the earliest days of America, however, that interpretation began to change. The seminal New England preachers Increase Mather and Cotton Mather, consumed by the literal zealotry of a once-persecuted congregation who were suddenly free to find their own way and their own ideas in the new world of the Bay Colony, reinterpreted 1 Thessalonians at face value, becoming the first Christians to articulate the idea that the faithful would literally be taken up into the air when Christ returned on Judgment Day. Though the Mathers's interpretation of 1 Thessalonians never caught on in their own day, a century and a half later the notion of Christ vacuuming up the faithful prior to the Tribulation would vault into the consciousness of millions of Christians in America, thanks to Darby and Scofield.

In 1827, Darby, living in Dublin, Ireland, began to develop a new brand of premillennialism known as *dispensationalism*. Rather than focusing on one or two scriptures of prophecy, as other apocalyptic preachers had done, Darby sought to weave the entire Bible together into one cohesive system, reasserting the inerrant authority of the Bible and promoting literal readings of the scriptures and prophecies.[18] Darby believed that the current age—the age, not incidentally, of science, empiricism, and progress—was the age of Satan; he believed that both the French and American Revolutions had been prophesied in the Bible, indicating that the end of the current age was at hand. But most importantly, Darby revived the literal interpretation of 1 Thessalonians of Increase and Cotton Mather; when the end finally came, Darby declared, the faithful would be Raptured up into the air.[19]

Darby's dispensationalism spread quickly among evangelicals in England, but it was in America, in the midst of the great premillennialist experimentation of the early nineteenth century, that dispensationalism found its most receptive audience. His ideas were quickly adopted or co-opted by the Millerites and Adventists, as well as by the Mormons, Pentecostals, and Jehovah's Witnesses. But Darby, observing the Great Disappointment of 1844, avoided getting caught up in the quagmire of date setting that had ensnared William Miller, even as he traveled the world promoting his new vision of the end of the age. He made at least six tours of the United States from 1859 to 1877. Preachers, Bible schools, and magazines spread the word of his vision, and dispensationalism increased its reach even further after Darby spoke at the Niagara Bible Conference at Niagara-on-the-Lake, Ontario, which James Brookes, Cyrus Scofield's mentor, had organized.[20]

But it would be Scofield who eventually vaulted Darby's revived idea of the Rapture beyond the new Christian sects and into mainstream American households. In 1909, he published *The Scofield Reference Bible*, the "Authorized Version," as the subtitle of the original Oxford University Press version puts it, "with a new system of connected topical references to all the greater themes of scripture."[21] Unlike previous Bible-study books that were published in separate volumes, Scofield innovatively placed his notes and commentary, which were based on the teachings of Darby's dispensationalism, next to the Bible passages themselves. The effect gave Scofield's own words and interpretations the same authority as the Bible itself, making the two almost indistinguishable and interchangeable; the result elevated Darby's ideas of a pre-Tribulation Rapture to the level of scripture in the minds of millions of evangelicals in America.[22]

The worldview found in *The Scofield Reference Bible* is fiercely anti-institutional and anti-government. It represents a scathing indictment of the Enlightenment ideal of progress; since humans are inherently flawed, and the world had been deteriorating since Christ's resurrection—since this is, in fact, the age of Satan—then all human creations are flawed as well. The followers of Darby and Scofield were determined to save souls rather than improve the world, which was beyond saving until Christ's Second Coming. They maintained that any social movement that hoped to alter the trajectory of humanity—to improve the status of slaves or women, or to rectify any number of social ills—was at best misguided, and at worst the devil's work. Scofield and his followers rejected science and technology on the same grounds, as human attempts to act as the Divine; they also dismissed Charles Darwin not simply for the obvious discrepancies between a literal interpretation of Genesis and evolution, but because they rejected the entire notion of progress. The righting of the state of world affairs, Scofield's readers were led to believe, should be left firmly in the hands of God, to take place after the Tribulation and Rapture.[23]

There has always been a separatist and reactive element to the most ardent of Christian apocalyptic beliefs. From the Essenes who left us the Dead Sea Scrolls to the earliest letters of the Apostle Paul, who urged his fellow Christians to renounce marriage and their responsibilities to the world from his dusty remote outpost on the fringes of the Roman Empire, those who have believed that the end of history was nigh have often retreated—physically, economically, intellectually, and spiritually—from the center of society. So, too, could the readers of *The Scofield Reference Bible*—which sold more than fifteen million copies during the twentieth century—retreat from the juggernaut of progress and secularism that was upending the traditional Christian world. They found solace in Darby and Scofield's declaration that all human science and endeavor—from evolution to women's rights—was folly.

FUNDAMENTALISM GOES NUCLEAR

While *The Scofield Reference Bible* introduced Darby's new vision of the end of the age to millions of American evangelicals, the Rapture's transformation into today's shorthand for the return of Christ would be complete only with the addition of another American invention—the atomic bomb.

Prior to Hiroshima and Nagasaki, the focal point of the apocalyptic expectation of most evangelical Christians—including Scofield and Darby—was less on Armageddon itself than on the kingdom on earth that would follow. While Armageddon had been vividly imagined by Christians for nearly two thousand years, it was the *mechanism* for bringing about God's kingdom on earth—a plot device, as it were, but hardly the point of the play.

The threat of nuclear annihilation, however, shifted the focus of apocalyptic anticipation from the world to come to the moment of its arrival. Nuclear apocalypse presented a metaphysical problem for those Christians who had yet to embrace Darby's vision of the

Rapture. After all, a nuclear apocalypse would be inescapable when it arrived—and more terrible than anyone had ever imagined. How could the faithful escape such a horrifying judgment, the type of judgment that burned the shadows of evaporated human beings onto the walls they had been walking beside only moments before? The Rapture solved the problem of a nuclear end to the world and the redemption of the faithful: believers would escape the destruction that all of creation could not, because Christ would pluck them out of the world in the moment before it was destroyed.[24]

Once the faithful had imagined their escape from a nuclear apocalypse through the Rapture, the threat of nuclear war became the vehicle of choice to increase attendance in fundamentalist pews throughout the Cold War. A prophetic writer by the name of Wilbur M. Smith is illustrative of a type of postnuclear Christian believer that most of us are familiar with—the type of person who would read the newspaper in one hand and the book of Revelation in the other, as Hal Lindsey once put it.[25]

Smith—who became enthralled by the apocalypse as a teenager after attending a conference at which Cyrus Scofield himself had spoken—swiftly and influentially wove the threat of nuclear annihilation into the fabric of Revelation, and into the ongoing argument between progress and apocalypse in America. Within six months of the end of the Second World War and the bombings of Hiroshima and Nagasaki, Smith produced a small booklet, *This Atomic Age and the Word of God*. Like Scofield before him, who had railed against the belief that technology and human ingenuity could better the human condition, Smith wrote that the bomb had "forced nonbelievers to consider seriously the claims of Biblical prophecy" and had put an end to the "foolish dreams" of secular progress. "Every act and plan and invention of godless man," he wrote, could only "hasten that day" in which God would destroy the earth. And like *The Scofield Reference Bible*, Smith's booklet was enormously influential; it was quickly condensed and published in *Reader's Digest*, where it reached millions of Americans, faithful and secular alike.[26]

For the next several decades, combining the threat of nuclear Armageddon with the return of Christ was like alchemy for a string of evangelical writers and preachers, producing real gold for those who juxtaposed Americans' new fear of a nuclear flash with biblical fire and brimstone. Hal Lindsey's *The Late Great Planet Earth*, which combined nuclear Armageddon with Soviet fear and hippie drug slang, sold millions of copies in the 1970s.[27] In the 1980s, as fear of a nuclear conflict with the Soviet Union reached new heights in America, the top televangelists of the day broadcast their own relentless sermons of apocalypse, insisting that the Tribulation was at hand. Jerry Falwell, who was a confidante of President Reagan, saw nuclear war as "inevitable, imminent, and (for most human beings) inescapable," in Paul Boyer's words.[28] And Pat Robertson, who would run for president himself later in the decade, so fervently believed that the Soviets would invade Israel and set off Armageddon that he declared in a May 1982 broadcast that "I guarantee you by the fall of 1982 there is going to be a judgment on the world."[29] By 1984, such rhetoric had convinced 39 percent of Americans that nuclear war had been prophesied in the Bible, according to one poll—with 25 percent believing that God would "spare them personally from the coming holocaust."[30] The Rapture had become nearly synonymous with the apocalypse in America, with a quarter of Americans believing the Rapture to be a central tenet of Christian scripture—though in fact it is an idea less than 170 years old, popularized barely more than a century ago by a one-time St. Louis jailbird.

THE BOMB WILL BRING US TOGETHER

During our own Apocalyptic Decade, all Americans over the age of thirty have shared, deep in the unspoken recesses of our collective unconscious, the terrifying understanding that the world could end at any moment in a nuclear firestorm. Even before most of us had been disabused of our belief in Santa Claus, those of us over a certain age had learned—whether through duck-and-cover drills in the 1950s or classroom discussions of the made-for-TV movie *The Day After* in the 1980s—that above our heads hung a nuclear sword of Damocles far beyond all reasoning or control. This nuclear fear is what has distinguished the apocalyptic imagination in the modern era from all of history, pushing the apocalypse from the realm of religion into the secular mainstream—a visceral shadow that has lingered at the edges of the modern imagination. It is not incidental that the postapocalyptic world envisioned in Cormac McCarthy's 2006 Pulitzer Prize–winning novel *The Road* is easily identifiable, though never explicitly confirmed, as a world beset by nuclear winter, with ashen-gray snow falling continuously from a sky so darkened by soot that no photosynthesis—no life— can exist beneath it. The gray world depicted in *The Road* has always been anticipated in the twilight of the modern era. To a degree that the generations who passed before 1945 could never understand, the nuclear age has made our expectation of apocalypse more visceral and universal than ever before.

Yet if Christian fundamentalists were able to weave the arrival of the nuclear age into their visions of apocalypse, the threat of nuclear annihilation presented those Americans who had long since dismissed the apocalypse as a primitive superstition—who had, like Charles Darwin, placed their faith in human or evolutionary progress, and "look[ed] with some confidence to a secure future of great length"[31]—with a deeper, more existential crisis. The dream of progress—of science, reason, and industry providing humanity with the means toward achieving a more perfect union on earth—exploded with the detonation of the first atomic bomb near Alamogordo, New Mexico. That dream of progress, which had been born in reaction to the apocalypse, was now forced to confront the apocalypse.

Of course, the belief in progress as an unadulterated good had already, decades earlier, collided with the realities of the twentieth century. Prior to 1914, as cultural historian Paul Fussell and others have argued, the belief in material and technological progress served as a substitute for religious belief in the secular mind;[32] the slaughter in the trenches during World War I, however, revealed the great chasm of spiritual emptiness that had widened beneath humanity as we marched so optimistically toward the future. If material and scientific progress could produce such horrors—and those horrors would increase as the twentieth century progressed—then what was the meaning of history, or of life itself? One could argue that the final answer rationalism would arrive at, now that god and myth had been displaced from creation (by Darwinism) and from history (by secular progress), was given to us by the existentialists: nothing. Life and history meant nothing.[33]

Thus, a sense of meaninglessness and cynicism had already crept into the American psyche between the world wars—"I'm pretty cynical about everything," Daisy declares in *The Great*

Gatsby, "I think everything's terrible anyhow. Everybody thinks so—the most advanced people."[34]—and even before the bomb had gone off, that sense of meaninglessness had begun to pervade and pervert the secular view of history. With neither a belief in progress nor a belief in an eschatological goal for history, the secular worldview by the early twentieth century raised the question: What was the point of it all?

That question was primarily an intellectual countercurrent, a literary theme confined to the intelligentsia and expatriate writers prior to 1945. But the atom bomb brought existential angst to the masses. Progress had emerged as an alternative to the apocalypse as a means of providing purpose to history; now, progress itself had led directly to an apocalypse on a scale that was previously unimaginable. The great detour away from the apocalyptic view of history through the secular faith in progress, which had begun with the rationalist thinkers after the Reformation and continued through the political revolutions of the eighteenth century and the industrial triumphs of the nineteenth century, had come to an end with the scientific achievements of the twentieth century. The bright promises of modernity and Darwin had been hollow. Science, which at the beginning of the Age of Enlightenment had promised to dispel the ghosts and demons of the medieval world, has instead become a propellant of the apocalyptic imagination. Man may have replaced God as the conductor of history in the secular mind, but the value and meaning of what he is conducting is, here at the beginning of the twenty-first century, very much in doubt.

The seeds of that doubt in progress were planted long before the atomic bomb, of course, and even before the horrors of the First World War. By the middle of the eighteenth century, Romanticism had arisen as a form of literary and intellectual revolt against the excesses of reason and the industrialization of the natural and human world. A sense that something spiritually important to humankind was being lost in the rush toward a secular golden future preoccupied the Victorian and Romantic poets in England. Matthew Arnold wrote mournfully of the "retreating sea of faith";[35] Tennyson feared "the secular abyss to come";[36] Thomas Hardy, in "God's Funeral," pondered "our myth's oblivion" and wondered "who or what shall fill his place?"[37] In America, the Transcendentalists claimed as the landscape of their own the vast territory between the church and the factory, rhapsodizing about nature while railing against both organized religion and the cost exacted by industry on the human soul. Who can forget Thoreau walking along the railroad tracks (to bring his laundry to be washed by his mother, as it turns out), imagining the railroad ties beneath the track as individual human lives, laid down for the expedience of progress? "Each one is a man, an Irishman, or a Yankee man. The rails are laid on them, and they are covered with sand, and the cars run smoothly over them. . . . And every few years a new lot is laid down and run over; so that, if some have the pleasure of riding on a rail, others have the misfortune to be ridden upon."[38]

The momentum of science would continue to propel us toward considerations of the end. In the twentieth century, science unveiled with startling rapidity new theories to describe the universe—from entropy to the big bang to mapping the great extinctions of past ages of life on earth—that consistently undermined the Enlightenment belief in a history progressing toward a more perfect state, with man as the conductor of the grand symphony. Consider, for example, the discovery in the late 1970s of the Chicxulub Crater in the Yucatán Peninsula, and the now commonly accepted understanding that a giant meteor strike some sixty-five million years ago caused the extinction of 90 percent of life on earth and the end of the Jurassic period.[39] Consider, too, that our understanding that such things as dinosaurs had ever even existed is barely more than a century and a half old. It was only around the time that Darwin was beginning to write *On the Origin of Species* that humanity first began to articulate the theory that the "dragon bones" that had been found throughout human history were in fact the fossilized remnants of dinosaurs and other creatures that lived millions of years ago. It took the rise of geology as a science, guided by the principle of uniformity, and the subsequent study of the fossil record—combined with the discovery of radiation in 1896, which later would allow scientists to begin accurately dating the ages of rocks and geologic formations—for humanity to formulate our present understanding that the earth's history can be divided into different eras and epochs, and that those eras and epochs had been punctuated by mass-extinction events. This understanding that the history of the earth has been marked by differing epochs of life—each of which were radically different from our present earth, and all of which ended rather abruptly and inconveniently for the dominant species of each era—is commonplace to us now; yet the notion would have seemed fantastical to even the most enlightened thinker just two hundred years ago. So, too, would our scientific understanding that all species—including humans—will eventually go extinct have sounded depressingly pessimistic and unthinkable. Yet this understanding that the history of the earth has been marked by mass-extinction events has been an important contributor to the secular apocalyptic impulse. Can humankind truly, in the space of forty years, or even one hundred and fifty, process what it means that the world has been radically different before and has changed drastically without warning or purpose? The geologic discoveries of the past century have upended our cosmology as radically as Copernicus's placement of the sun—rather than the earth—at the center of the solar system; the metaphysical implications of both discoveries have yet to be synthesized in our cosmology.

Indeed, rather than killing off apocalyptic beliefs with reason, the advances of science and technology have exacerbated apocalyptic anxiety by giving birth to more scenarios that could produce the end times, from meteor strikes and epidemic disease to global warming.[40] Here, at last, is the modern apocalypse, the secular apocalypse, an anticipation of the end that touches believer and nonbeliever alike. For many, the arrival of the world wars and then the atomic bomb—and, now, global warming, overpopulation, and resource depletion—has permanently shattered humanity's faith in secular and scientific progress as a substitute for religious and mythical meaning.

Or, put another way, the twenty-first century has arrived.

CHAPTER 5

THE APOCALYPSE WILL TAKE A LITTLE WHILE

Flip through the cable channels for long enough, and you'll inevitably find the apocalypse. On channels like Discovery or Nature or History you'll find shows like *MegaDisasters*, *Armageddon*, or *The Last Days on Earth* chronicling, in an hour of programming, dozens of ways the world might end: a gamma ray burst from a nearby star peeling away the Earth's ozone layer like an onion; a mega-volcano erupting and plunging our planet into a new ice age; the magnetic poles reversing. Turn to a news channel, and the headlines appear equally apocalyptic, declaring that the "UN Warns of Rapid Decay in Environment" or that "Humanity's Very Survival" is at risk or that a recent United Nations Environment Programme's Global Environment Outlook report is a "final wake-up call" to the world. On another station, you'll find some people arguing that the true apocalyptic threat to our way of life is not the impending collapse of ecosystems and biodiversity but the collapse of the dollar as the world's global currency. Change the channel again, and you'll see still others insisting that malarial mosquitoes, drunk on West Nile virus, are the looming specter of apocalypse darkening our nation's horizon. Hit the clicker a final time, and you'll again find alarmists reaching into the scientific grab bags of paleogeology and astronomy to demonstrate that if super-volcanism doesn't send all of us the way of Pompeii, then a gigantic asteroid is virtually guaranteed to smack our planet upside the head and bring all mammalian life to a sudden end.

How to make sense of it all? After all, not every scenario can be an apocalyptic threat to our way of life—can it? For many—remembering the nonevent of Y2K and numbed by the apocalyptic sensationalism with which the media reports so many stories—the tendency is to dismiss *all* the crises we are facing as overblown, to fall back into that Y2K dismissal mode of hoax or hype. Perhaps cap and trade is just a smoke screen designed to earn Al Gore billions from his clean-energy investments; perhaps terrorism is just an excuse to increase the power and reach of the government. For others, the panoply of potential disasters becomes overwhelming, leading to a distorted and paranoid vision of reality and the threats facing our world. Will an epidemic wipe out humanity, or could a meteor destroy all life on earth? By the time you're done watching "Armageddon Week" on the History Channel, even a rapid reversal of the world's magnetic poles might seem terrifyingly likely and imminent.

The last time apocalyptic anxiety spilled into the mainstream to the extent that it altered the course of history—during the Reformation—it relied on a revolutionary new communications technology: the printing press. In a similar way, could the current surge in apocalyptic anxiety be attributed in part to our own revolution in communications technology? Certainly the proliferation of cable news in the late 1980s and '90s and the growth of the Internet during the 2000s have created not simply more "choice" for news consumers; they have created a vacuum of content that needs to be filled. For example, in the three and a half decades prior to the launch of CNN in 1980, the "Big 3" networks—ABC, CBS, and NBC—programmed little more than three hours of news per day, with the vast majority of that programming consumed by morning lifestyle and entertainment reports aimed at stay-at-home mothers. The launch of the first twenty-four-hour news channel created an insatiable need for more content—a need that grew voraciously as competitors to CNN (from Fox News to MSNBC to CNBC) entered the marketplace. The growth of twenty-four-hour news in the 1990s helps explain why coverage of violent crime increased by 600 percent in that decade, even as the actual rate of violent crime fell by 20 percent over the same period.[1] That proliferation of media channels has, of course, only accelerated with the rapid growth of the Internet, which has brought us a phalanx of blogs, aggregators, and video channels hungry for content that must be ever-more dramatic to attract a sliver of an increasingly distracted and overstimulated audience.[2]

The media, of course, have long mastered the formula of packaging remote possibilities as urgent threats, as sociologist Barry Glassner pointed out in his bestseller *The Culture of Fear*. We're all familiar with the formula: "It's worse than you think," the anchor intones before delivering an alarming report on date-rape drugs, stalking pedophiles, flesh-eating bacteria, the Ebola virus (née avian flu cum swine flu). You name it (or rename it): if a threat has even a remote chance of materializing, it is treated as an imminent inevitability by television news. It's not just that if it bleeds, it leads. If it *might* bleed, it still leads. Such sensationalist speculation attracts eyeballs and sells advertising, because fear sells—and it can sell everything from pharmaceuticals to handguns to duct tape to insurance policies. Glassner notes the observation of Richard Nixon to illustrate the point that vast amounts of money can be made by those who stoke our collective anxiety: "People react to fear, not love," Nixon once said. "They don't teach that in Sunday school, but it's true."[3]

Nothing inspires fear like the end of the world, and ever since Y2K, the media's tendency toward overwrought speculation has been increasingly married to the rhetoric of apocalypse. Today, nearly any event can be explained through apocalyptic language, from birds falling out of the sky (the Birdocalypse?) to a major nor'easter (Snowmageddon!) to a double-dip recession (Barackalypse! Obamageddon!). Armageddon is here at last—and your local news team is live on the scene! We've seen the equivalent of grade inflation (A for Apocalypse!) for every social, political, or ecological challenge before us, an escalating game of one-upmanship to gain the public's attention. Why worry about global warming and rising sea levels when the collapse of the housing bubble has already put your mortgage underwater? Why worry that increasing droughts will threaten the supply of drinking water in America's major cities when a far greater threat lies in the possibility of an Arab terrorist poisoning that drinking supply, resulting in millions of casualties? Yet not all of the crises or potential threats before us are equal, nor are they equally probable—a fact that gets glossed over when the media equate the remote threat of a possible event, like epidemics, with real trends like global warming.

APOCALYPSE DU JOUR

When it comes to reporting on potential apocalyptic threats, few scenarios have had as much resiliency for journalists and anchors than the nebulous threat of a global pandemic.

We're all familiar with the steady stream of diseases that have been hawked by television newscasters over the past ten years. Like an endless series of stock characters on a sitcom that has long since grown stale, the names constantly change—from West Nile Virus to SARS to Ebola to avian flu—but the story does not; the fear of the unseen, of diseases with rapid incubation rates, is conjured with striking regularity by any anchorperson with a breathless lead. If one were to judge the probability of apocalypse solely on the basis of airtime on television news, global epidemics would rank as one of the greatest threats to our way of life.

But are epidemics really capable of bringing about the world's end? The majority of diseases trumpeted by the media as apocalyptic are rather weak in historical terms and are not quite ready for prime time. Yet by confusing what is possible with what is probable, the media often report the worst-case scenario as an imminent threat. To become a pandemic, for example, avian flu would have to evolve to change its primary vector, or means of transmission, first from bird to bird, then from to bird to human, and finally from human to human. In the midst of this evolutionary whirlwind, it would also have to maintain not only its lethality (currently about 50 percent when it does strike humans) but also its longevity (its ability to live long enough to kill its host) and its virality (the ability to replicate from host to host), as well. It's certainly possible for avian flu to successfully navigate so many winnowing gates to become a major killer of human beings, but doing so is the evolutionary equivalent of winning a Powerball® ticket. It is strikingly rare, scientists will tell you, for diseases to achieve and maintain all the criteria necessary to become a pandemic—which is one reason why actual global pandemics are few and far between.[4]

The infrequency with which a virus successfully runs this evolutionary gamut is usually buried beneath provocative headlines.

Take, for example, a 2006 article that ran originally in the
Guardian but was picked up by papers throughout the United
States and across the English-speaking world. Titled "Bird Flu
Could Be 21st-Century Black Death," this special report raised the
specter of a societal breakdown on the scale last seen in the mid-
fourteenth century, when the Plague swept through Western
Europe. Once you read past the headline, however, you discover
that "there [is] only a small risk of a return to the economic and
social chaos caused by the Black Death, and it would only occur if
bird flu conflated with other risks to the global community."[5] In
other words, while avian flu *could* bring about the end of the world,
it would require a lot of help from its friends, such as a simulta-
neous economic crash that curtailed the ability to provide preventive care. Indeed, what historical analogies to past pandemics often
fail to take into account are new advances in modern medicine or
the degree to which governments, nongovernmental organiza-
tions, and scientists are prepared to respond to a pandemic outbreak today. This capacity to respond to an emerging crisis is often
overlooked when the media report on the threat of epidemics.

The media also overlook the actual impact of a global outbreak
of disease. Consider, for example, the last great global pandemic:
the Spanish flu outbreak of 1918. In just more than eighteen
months, the Spanish flu killed between fifty to one hundred million
people worldwide, or up to 3 percent of the global population—
more people than were killed in World War I. But like any pandemic, it relied on extraordinary circumstances: the millions of soldiers waiting to be shipped home following the end of the First
World War provided the Spanish flu with a dense population, living
in cramped, shared quarters, allowing this particularly virulent
strain to spread rapidly. Within six months, the virus had infected

up to a third of the world's population, killing between 10 and 20 percent of those infected. Yet a year later, the virus disappeared entirely; the same evolutionary bonanza that had allowed it to become so lethal so quickly had continued until, scientists now suspect, it evolved into a less lethal strain of influenza. The Spanish flu probably contributed to the post–World War I recessions that hung over the world as the second decade of the twentieth century drew to a close; yet Americans in particular rebounded from the effects of World War I and the Spanish flu with a renewed optimism and exuberance, setting the tone for the Roaring Twenties.

Even in their most devastating form, pandemics don't end the world—though they can radically change it. Consider the most famous and deadly pandemic in history: the Black Death, which spread through Europe in the fourteenth century and killed between twenty and thirty million Europeans, or between one-third to two-thirds of Europe's total population. More than one-fifth of the world's population (approximately 450 million at the time) likely died in the pandemic, and it would take nearly 150 years for the global population to recover from the catastrophic effects of the Plague.[6]

Like the Spanish flu of the early twentieth century, the Black Death of the fourteenth century required help from extraordinary circumstances—including famine and a rapidly changing climate—to achieve its devastating results. In the three hundred years prior to the Black Death, Europe's population had nearly doubled, thanks in large part to technological and agricultural advancements such as the heavy plow. By the end of the thirteenth century, however, the world's climate began to shift: the Medieval Warm Period, which began around 950 CE and allowed European harvests to blossom (along with the population), gave way to a period known today as the Little Ice Age. The price of food soared as harvests decreased in the face of colder temperatures, and shortages of grains grew widespread, especially in northern Europe. The Great Famine of 1315–1317 resulted, reducing the European population by as much as 10 percent.[7]

By the time the Plague arrived in southern Italy in 1347 (it had originated in China the century before, spread by the Mongol hordes and killing up to half of the Chinese population over several decades), it found a weakened population still reeling from climate change and the lingering effects of famine. Within eight months, the Plague had spread to Spain, Portugal, France, and England; within a year, it had returned east to decimate the populations of Germany, Scandinavia, Poland, and Russia, eventually making its way to the Middle East before finally subsiding in 1350.

The swiftness with which the Plague struck Europe caused a complete breakdown in social order, especially in the mercantilist cities that were hardest hit by a disease that spread rapidly via major trade routes. The centers of social, economic, and political power weakened; religion faltered; corruption soon abounded in local governments. Those who survived faced a radically changed world. With so many dead, the price of land collapsed—many land-owning families were wiped out of existence, leaving their properties without heirs—while the value of labor (and soon wages) soared. In the decades that followed, per capita wealth in Europe rose dramatically, and soon innovations in technology—from the printing press to the windmill—came to market to support the growing middle class that had emerged in the wake of *Yersinia pestis*. In the long run, the Plague—by breaking the feudalist structure that relied on a concentration of wealth and land ownership as well as the cheap labor of a rapidly growing population—led not to the apocalypse but to the Renaissance.[8]

Rather than looking to the Plague to understand what the trajectory of a pandemic outbreak in the twenty-first century might look like, we need only look to the most recent pandemic to strike the modern world: AIDS, which has killed twenty-five million people in just over twenty-five years. When it first appeared in the popular consciousness in the mid-1980s, HIV generated much of the irrational and hyperbolic fear that we see today in media coverage of avian flu or swine flu. Despite its ease of transmission, lethality, and long incubation period—a trifecta that any virus would love to hit—much of the developed world has escaped the devastation that AIDS could have caused, not only because of advances in care and medicine but also because of effective public education and prevention campaigns. Where the disease has been most ravaging, such as in Africa, it has relied on a great deal of support from illiteracy, poverty, and war.

The probability that any of the diseases portrayed apocalyptically by the media could evolve into a global pandemic that truly threatens the world is, from an evolutionary and medical perspective, extraordinarily slim. Medical science has advanced tremendously, and our ability to treat secondary infections such as pneumonia or strep throat (which contributed significantly to the death rate of the Spanish flu of 1918) is significantly higher. Our early-warning mechanisms for the outbreak of disease, as well, are better prepared to sound the alarm; the media's hyping of every potential outbreak of avian flu or SARS or swine flu in the last decade is evidence that pandemics are capable of reliably getting more press than Britney Spears or Lindsay Lohan. And without discounting the massive human suffering that such outbreaks present, on a historical scale the evidence suggests that global pandemics, in the rare instances that they do occur, don't end the world—they renew it.

EVENTS VERSUS TRENDS

But epidemics are only one apocalyptic media darling. Over the last decade, the twenty-four-hour news cycle and the proliferation of media channels has created ever-more apocalyptic content that is readily available to us, from images of the Twin Towers falling in 2001 to images of the Japanese tsunami in 2011. So, too, have cable channels like Discovery and History married advances in computer-generated imagery with emerging scientific understanding of our planet and universe to give visual validity to the rare and catastrophic events that have occurred in the past or that may take place in the distant future. Using dramatic, animated images and the language of apocalypse to peddle such varied scenarios, however, has the effect of leveling the apocalyptic playing field, leaving the viewer with the impression that terrorism, bird flu, global warming, and asteroids are all equally probable. But not all of these apocalyptic scenarios are equally likely, and they're certainly not equally likely to occur within our lifetimes—or in our neighborhoods. For example, after millions of Americans witnessed the attacks of 9/11 on television, our collective fear of terrorism was much higher than its actual probability; in 2001, terrorists killed one-twelfth as many Americans as did the flu and one-fifteenth as many Americans as did car accidents.[9] Throughout the first decade of the twenty-first century, the odds of an American being killed by a terrorist were about 1 in 88,000—compared to a 1 in 10,010 chance of dying from falling off a ladder.[10] The fears of an outbreak of SARS, avian flu, or swine flu also never lived up to their media hype.

This overreliance on the apocalyptic narrative causes us to fear the wrong things and to mistakenly equate potential future events with current and observable trends. How to discern the difference between so many apocalyptic options? If we ask ourselves three basic questions about the many threats portrayed apocalyptically in the media, we are able to separate the apocalyptic wheat from the chaff. Which scenarios are probable? Which are preventable? And what is the likely impact of the worst-case model of any given threat?

In answering these questions, it becomes clear that much of what the media peddles as apocalyptic is not. The apocalyptic scenarios involving global disaster—from meteor impacts to super-volcanic eruptions—are extraordinarily rare. An asteroid *could* hit the Earth and lead to the extinction of all mammals, including us, but the geologic record tells us that such massive strikes are unlikely, and logic tells us that there is little we can do to prevent one. Nor are terrorist attacks or an outbreak of avian flu likely to destroy humanity; their impact is relatively small and usually localized, because we can be prepared for such threats and can contain and mitigate their effects. The apocalyptic storyline tells us that most of these events are probable, largely unpreventable, and destined to be catastrophic. But none of this is true—their probability is either low or can be made lower through preventive means, or their impact is containable. (The degree of damage caused by Hurricane Katrina, for example, could have been minimized through better preparation both in infrastructure and in the government's response. Yet even without such preparations, the impact remained relatively localized.)

The danger of the media's conflation of apocalyptic scenarios is that it leads us to believe that our existential threats come exclusively from events that are beyond our control and that await us in the future—and that a moment of universal recognition of such threats will be obvious to everyone when they arrive. No one, after all, would ever confuse a meteor barreling toward Earth as anything other than apocalyptic. Yet tangled up in such Hollywood scenarios and sci-fi nightmares are actual threats that aren't arriving in an instant of universal recognition; instead, they are arriving amid much denial and continued partisan debate. For example, annual climate-related disasters such as droughts, storms, and floods rose dramatically during the Apocalyptic Decade, increasing an average 75 percent compared to the 1990s—just as many climate models predicted they would if global warming were left unchecked.[11] Yet this rise in natural disasters hasn't produced a moment of universal recognition of the dangers of climate change; instead, belief in climate change is actually on the decline as we adjust to the "new normal" of ever-weirder weather or convince ourselves that our perception of this increased frequency is a magnifying trick of more readily available cable and Internet coverage.

Despite the media's best efforts to conflate them with improbable scenarios, the existential challenges that we must confront in the twenty-first century don't fit into the apocalyptic storyline of future cataclysmic events that are beyond our control—because they aren't truly *events* but rather are *trends*. Whether or not we will be able to control them hinges on our understanding that the moment of revelation doesn't lie before us in some indeterminate future—it is already here.

BELIEVE IT OR NOT

Of the many challenges facing us at the beginning of the twenty-first century, none has become more entangled with apocalyptic rhetoric than global warming.

From the beginning, the threat of climate change has been

painted in apocalyptic colors. A full quarter century ago, during the swelteringly hot summer of 1988—a summer of interminable drought that devastated crops in the American heartland and caused the waters of the Mississippi to fall so low that barge traffic on the river literally ground to a halt—James Hansen, director of NASA's Goddard Institute for Space Studies, made his way up the steps of the Capitol to testify before the US Senate. Armed with a compendium of computer models, temperature measurements, and GIS maps, Hansen meticulously unveiled the scientific evidence that indicated that the massive amounts of CO_2 being released by humankind, primarily through the use of fossil fuels, was fundamentally altering the earth's climate.

Hansen wasn't the first scientist to be concerned about the impact of industry and the burning of fossil fuels on the earth's climate. As early as 1938, a British steam engineer and inventor by the name of Guy Stewart Callendar had put forward the theory that the burning of fossil fuels was releasing enough carbon dioxide into the atmosphere to warm the earth. Although Callendar viewed such warming as beneficial, his theory was roundly dismissed, largely because most scientists believed that the actions of humankind were too miniscule to alter a system as large as the global climate.[12]

By the 1950s and '60s, however, the assumption that humankind's actions had little impact on vast and complex systems began to rapidly break down. "Killer smogs" produced by industrial pollution descended on London, Los Angeles, and New York, killing hundreds in America and up to 12,000 in London. In 1962, Rachel Carson's *Silent Spring* convinced millions of readers around the globe that the widespread use of pesticides such as DDT was devastating natural ecosystems and jeopardizing human health. By the 1970s, the idea that the actions of humankind were too trivial to impact ecosystems on a massive and devastating scale had evaporated—burned up, as it were, by the fires on the Cuyahoga River in northeast Ohio. Any residual doubt about our ability to impact the environment on a planetary scale was eradicated in 1985 with the discovery that CFCs—chlorofluorocarbons, released primarily through aerosol sprays and refrigerators—were burning a hole in the ozone layer, which absorbs most of the sun's deadly ultraviolet radiation. This discovery led to a relatively prompt global agreement to ban the use of the damaging compounds. Thus, by the time James Hansen ascended the steps of the US Capitol on that hot summer day in 1988, an entire generation of Americans had grown up with a deeply suspect view of modern industry and technology. That the excesses of both could inadvertently ruin the world was now a matter of mainstream modern memory, rather than obscure scientific speculation.

There isn't an American alive today who couldn't give you a CliffsNotes® version of the consequences that Hansen warned the Senate about that day if this growth in CO_2 emissions was left unchecked. If humankind did nothing to stop it, Hansen warned, the greenhouse effect would cause the polar ice caps to melt, raising sea levels that would swamp the great ports and cities of civilization; increased hurricane activity and severe droughts would devastate global agriculture, leading to starvation and dislocation for millions; the stability of the climate that had allowed civilization to flourish for the last 12,000 years would disappear. At the end of his hair-raising testimony, Hansen declared that he and many of his fellow scientists were "99 percent sure . . . that the [human-caused] greenhouse effect has been detected and it is changing our climate now."[13]

Hansen's apocalyptic vision of climate change captured the world's imagination during a summer in which "super" Hurricane Gilbert—the largest Atlantic hurricane on record—smashed into Mexico; massive wildfires in the Amazon consumed millions of acres of rain forest; and graphic and heart-wrenching images of Yellowstone National Park ablaze were beamed into the living rooms of an increasingly anxious nation.[14] One can pick almost any year in the past quarter century to find similar examples of worsening and ever-weirder weather, from Hurricane Katrina to devastating floods and droughts across the continent to the melting of the polar ice caps that Hansen and his fellow scientists warned us with "99 percent" certainty would be the result of unhindered climate change some twenty-five years ago. So, too, can one point to dozens of major scientific reports that illustrate the growing alarm among scientists that Hansen's original dire predictions weren't dire enough and that the pace of global climate change had, if anything, been underestimated in the earliest studies.

And yet today in America, belief in global warming is actually in decline, with only 59 percent of adults in 2010 believing there is solid evidence of human-caused climate change, compared to 79 percent in 2006. Beneath those numbers lies an increasing partisan divide between believers and nonbelievers, with only 16 percent of Republicans in 2010 believing that climate change is caused by human activity.[15] How did this reversal in the belief in global warming happen despite the mounting scientific and firsthand evidence? How did we go from 99 percent certainty among scientists in 1988 to just 16 percent belief among conservatives in 2010? What caused so many Americans to ignore the mounting evidence before their eyes and turn global warming from a debate about scientific evidence to a question of personal belief?

The answer lies in part with the disinformation campaign mounted almost immediately after Hansen's testimony before Congress in the summer of 1988 by the oil, gas, coal, and automotive industries. Borrowing from the playbook of the tobacco industry, which had fought for decades to conceal the true health effects of smoking, the fossil fuel and automotive industries and the public utilities would, over the next two decades, invest billions of dollars in setting up their own think tanks and astroturf front groups (such as the Global Climate Coalition and the Information Council on the Environment) in an effort to obfuscate the growing scientific consensus around climate change and to derail political efforts to address the issue.[16]

The earliest line of attack pursued by the global-warming deniers was to question the scientific consensus, arguing that there was too much disagreement among climate scientists to warrant bold action. More studies were needed, the industry reps insisted. When more studies showed a growing scientific certainty that global warming was happening, the industry front groups tried to spin the effects of global warming as a positive that would expand agricultural production and lessen the threat of harsh winters to the poor and elderly in the Northern Hemisphere.[17] Global warming *might* be real, the industry front groups conceded, but it was *good* for you. CO_2, after all, is the very thing that plants and trees use to create their bounteous harvest for humanity. Those who were afraid of carbon dioxide were misguided alarmists; as one television advertisement declared about CO_2: "They call it pollution. We call it life."[18] When that argument became unsustainable against broadcast images of glaciers calving into the Arctic Ocean, the industry front groups turned to solar flares as an alternative explanation for a process that even they could no longer deny was taking place. Global warming was real, they'd been forced to concede; its effects would be disastrous, they finally admitted; but perhaps the matter was wholly out of our hands. The industry reps advocated a reversal of the precautionary principle: since we couldn't be sure that global warming was caused by carbon emissions, we should do nothing until we had greater certainty. As one political cartoonist put it at the end of the Apocalyptic Decade, what if we took the necessary steps to move toward a clean-energy economy—only to find out that global warming was a hoax and we'd created a better world for nothing?[19]

To understand why we haven't created that better world in the past quarter century—despite the mounting scientific evidence that climate change is real, caused by human use of fossil fuels, and rapidly accelerating beyond our control—we must look beyond the industry-funded movement to deny the reality and effects of climate change. Perhaps equally important—if not quite equally culpable—has been the extent to which both the proponents and opponents of human-made climate change have led us down a cul-de-sac of conversation by exploiting the apocalyptic metaphor to make their case.

Whether by design or by accident, the initial warnings of Hansen and others—of oceans rising to engulf our most beloved metropolises, of amber waves of grain scorched into a desert landscape—activated the apocalyptic impulse. The focus on disastrous repercussions for our behavior at some point in the future echoed the warnings of the Israelite priests to wayward Jews in Babylon or, later, to those who submitted too willingly to Alexander's process of Hellenization. It was a familiar story: change, and change radically, or face hell on earth. Perhaps there was no other way to sound the alarm about the devastating threat presented by global climate change, but that echo of apocalyptic warning was quickly seized upon by the opponents of global warming to dismiss the evidence out of hand. We've heard this story before, the deniers insisted, and throughout history those who have declared the end of the world was near have always been proven wrong. As early as 1989, the industry front man Patrick Michaels, a climatologist and global-warming skeptic, was warning in the op-ed pages of the *Washington Post* of this new brand of "apocalyptic environmentalism," which represented "the most popular new religion to come along since Marxism."[20] That the solutions to global warming (a less carbon-intensive economy, a more localized trade system, a greater respect for nature's power) parallel so perfectly the dream of environmentalists, and that the causes of global warming (an unrestrained industrial capitalism reliant on the continued and accelerating consumption of fossil fuels) parallel the economic dream of conservatives, has simply exacerbated the fact that global warming has now become just another front in the culture wars. By seizing upon and mocking the apocalyptic imagery and rhetoric of those sounding the alarm, the industry front groups succeeded in framing the debate about global warming into a question about what one *believes*.

Thus, entangled with the myth of apocalypse—and its attendant hold on our own sense of belief and self-identity—the debate about anthropogenic climate change has reached an impasse. You believe in the Rapture; I believe in global warming—and so the conversation stops. But global climate change is not an apocalyptic event that will take place in the future; it is a human-caused trend that is occurring now. And as we expend more time either fearfully imagining or vehemently denying whether that trend will bring about a future apocalypse, scientists tell us that the trend is accelerating.

THE END OF EASY OIL

Global warming isn't the only observable trend to become entangled in the apocalyptic storyline during the past decade. As temperatures soared throughout the early 2000s, the price of oil also soared—bringing the idea of global peak oil and its attendant apocalyptic scenarios into the public consciousness.

There is virtually nothing we use in our daily lives that has not been transformed by the input of oil. Drive to the store, purchase some beef from Argentina and some potatoes from Idaho, and then go home, cook your steak on the grill, and turn on your iPod® while you enjoy your meal. Everything you will have touched during such an idle evening will have literally been made from oil: the car, the fuel in the tank, the road you drove on, the corn that was grown to feed the cow, the tractor that planted and then harvested your potatoes, the propane in your grill, the plastic of your iPod and speakers.

Oil isn't merely another form of energy; it is *the* form of energy that has made the modern world possible. The very basis of our economic system—which relies on continuous, exponential growth—has been possible because we have had a cheap, plentiful, and extraordinarily efficient form of energy—oil—at our disposal. Oil has allowed us to continue to eat despite the massive explosion in world population during the last century—from just 1.5 billion in 1900 to more than 7 billion today—because oil allowed not just the mechanization of agriculture but the development and application of the fertilizers and pesticides that have exponentially increased the productive yields of arable lands to feed our burgeoning population. (As physics educator A. A. Bartlett succinctly put it, "Modern agriculture is the use of land to convert petroleum into food."21) Oil, as others have observed, was a one-time gift from the gods, a gift that has allowed each of us to live like emperors, capable of traveling vast distances on a whim or conjuring forth goods and delicacies and information from around the world at a moment's notice, and at affordable prices.

But oil is a finite resource, and the evidence of global peak oil suggests that the period during which we could rely on expanding production of that resource to fuel the continued growth of the global economy is coming to an end—if it's not already behind us.

The scientific basis for peak oil has been intrinsically understood since the days of the first wildcatters. Wherever you drill an oil well, either pressure in the rock or mechanical assistance (such as a pump) will bring the oil up out of the ground at a rate that increases until it reaches a maximum peak—a peak that is limited by either the pressure forcing the oil up or the extraction rate of the pump. You can increase the rate of extraction through various means—by using a larger pump, for example, or by forcing water or gas into nearby rock to increase the pressure that forces the oil out—but inevitably a peak is reached, followed by a plateau in production. This plateau may last a long or a short time, but eventually and inevitably the rate of production will begin to decline. This rate of decline can be sudden, and the well can quickly run dry; or the rate of decline can be slow, allowing the well to continue producing oil at a much slower rate for years to come. The oldest continuously producing oil well in the country, for example—the McClintock Number 1 well, drilled in 1861 just 240 yards away from the famous Drake Well, which had launched the global oil industry two years earlier near Titusville, Pennsylvania—at one time produced a peak of fifty barrels of oil per day. One hundred and fifty years later, McClintock Number 1 can still produce one barrel of oil per day, though that oil is largely mixed with brine. (The Drake Well, in comparison, went completely dry in just two years.)

Building on such observations of the decline of oil and natural gas fields, a geologist by the name of M. King Hubbert gave a startling presentation in 1956 to the American Petroleum Institute in San Antonio, Texas. Hubbert had observed that the production life of all oil fields resembles a bell curve: the production rate of any given oil field eventually reaches a peak—a point at which the maximum flow of oil from the reserve has been reached—and then declines at roughly the same rate that it had risen, until the individual oil field is depleted.

Hubbert's bell curve meshed with the experiences of the oilmen who had gathered in San Antonio in 1956—but it was his extrapolation of what that bell curve meant that caused controversy. What is true for an individual oil field would prove true for national oil production as a whole, Hubbert contended. Based on his analysis of known reserves throughout the United States, as well as the fact that large new oil field discoveries were becoming increasingly rare by 1954 (the rate of new discoveries would begin to permanently decline a decade later, in 1964), and assuming that the consumption of oil would continue to rise at existing rates, Hubbert contended that the United States would reach a point of peak oil production sometime between the late 1960s and the early 1970s. After that point, barring unforeseeable and miraculous discoveries of new oil fields, domestic production of oil in the United States would reach a state of perpetual and irreversible decline.[22]

Hubbert turned out to be right. American oil production peaked in 1970, when domestic oil production topped out at 9.6

million barrels per day. Despite millions of acres of public land and miles of shoreline opened up to drilling, and despite major advances in drilling techniques and technology, American oil production has been in perpetual decline ever since. We now produce about 5.5 million barrels of crude per day, or about the same amount that we produced in the late 1940s.[23] The ramifications of domestic peak oil became obvious with the OPEC (Organization of Petroleum Exporting Countries) oil embargo of 1973: America's new reliance on imported oil radically reshaped global politics and led directly to the Carter Doctrine, which declared that any attempt by an outside force to gain control of the Persian Gulf region would be regarded as an attack on the vital interests of the United States.

Yet peak oil wasn't simply an American problem. If Hubbert's peak theory was true for any given oil field and had been demonstrated to be true for oil production in the United States, then it would eventually become true for the world as a whole: global oil production would also reach a peak, to be followed by a permanent decline in world oil production. For much of the 1980s and '90s, however, that global peak appeared to be a long way off. Massive discoveries of oil in the 1970s and 1980s—in the North Sea, at Prudhoe Bay, and at the Cantarell Field in Mexico—flooded the world with cheap oil. This deluge of cheap oil reversed the successful conservation efforts that Americans had implemented in response to the oil shocks of the 1970s, giving rise to the age of the SUV and sending the price of oil plummeting. (It bottomed at an inflation-adjusted $16 per barrel in January of 1999.)

It was about this time that a slew of geologists, journalists, and writers began to raise the alarm that the peak of *global* oil production was fast approaching—with many writers arguing that the consequences would be apocalyptic to our industrial way of life. Decades of globalization and a rising standard of living in countries like China and India meant demand was increasing rapidly, yet the rate of discovery of new oil fields was in decline around the world. Eventually the moment of truth would arrive, when global production couldn't keep up with demand—and that moment of truth was often painted in deeply apocalyptic terms. Journalist Bryant Urstadt summarized the vision of those who believe peak oil portends the apocalypse:

> The economy will begin an endless contraction, a prelude to the "grid crash." Cars will revert to being a luxury item, isolating the suburban millions from food and goods. Industrial agriculture will wither, addicted as it is to natural gas for fertilizer and to crude oil for flying, shipping, and trucking its produce. International trade will halt, leaving the Walmarts empty. In the United States, Northern homes will be too expensive to heat and Southern homes will roast. Dirty alternatives such as coal and tar sands will act as a bellows to the furnace of global warming. In response to all of this, extreme political movements will form, and the world will devolve into a fight to control the last of the resources. Whom the wars do not kill starvation will. Man, if he survives, will do so in agrarian villages.[24]

Such jeremiads have been countered by that old antidote to apocalyptic thinking: our belief in progress. This shared belief that progress will overcome the problem of peak oil is masked by a seemingly partisan debate: those on the left argue that alternative energy sources will seamlessly rise up to replace declining oil production and allow us to continue our way of life; while those on the right, elucidating a twenty-first-century version of the nineteenth-century belief that the rain follows the plow, argue that if we simply open up more areas offshore and on our public lands, then we'll have more than enough oil to continue our industrial way of life for centuries to come. Thus, like global warming, peak oil has departed the realm of scientific inquiry and economic analysis to become a question of personal belief. Do you believe in progress, or do you believe the End Is Near? Can't we just dismiss those naysayers who believe we'd all be sent back to the Stone Age by a rapid decline in global oil production? All we have to do is believe in the power of technology and human ingenuity, and everything will be alright.

Whenever we get caught between apocalyptic pronouncements that the world is ending and the knee-jerk response that it's not, we invariably fall into the trap of simplistic thinking and thus fail to grasp the challenges that we must confront. But when you divorce the problem of global peak oil from both the apocalyptic storyline and a blind faith in progress, the issue of peak oil—and its implications—becomes easier to understand.

Broadly speaking, most geologists believe that we have used approximately half of the world's oil reserves in the past century or so of modern living. At first glance, that would seem to imply that we have another century or more before we have to worry about running out of oil. But the last century hasn't been very equitable in its distribution of access to easy energy; while Western and developed nations were the primary consumers of the first half of that gift from the gods, the rising industrial appetites of the so-called BRIC countries (Brazil, Russia, India, and China) are demanding greater access to the second half. Rising global demand and the law of exponential growth suggest that we will burn through that second half of the world's oil reserves at a constantly accelerating rate. But the problem of peak oil isn't simply a question of when we run completely out of oil—that moment is at least fifty years away.[25] The question that peak oil forces us to confront more immediately is this: What happens when the rate of oil production can't keep up with global demand?

We may already be witnessing the answer to that question. In the first five years of the new millennium, oil prices climbed steadily through $40, $50, and $60 per barrel, yet global demand continued to rise unabated. In 2005, total world production of crude oil reached a plateau of about seventy-four million barrels per day. Then, the world watched as the price of oil went parabolic, reaching $100 per barrel in January of 2008. Yet this quintupling of the price of oil in just nine years was only the beginning: over the next seven months, the price of oil continued to soar to previously unimaginable heights, peaking at just over $147 per barrel in July of 2008. This surge in energy costs played a considerable role in triggering the global economic meltdown that confronted the world in the autumn of 2008. Only when global demand for oil retracted (demand decreased by nearly 10 percent in the United States over the next two years) did the surge in oil prices finally abate, plummeting in a classic case of overcorrection to just $38 per barrel in March of 2009. By the spring of 2011, however—despite the lingering global recession and unemployment in America stuck near 9 percent—the price of oil had rebounded to above $100 per barrel—a sevenfold increase from just a dozen years earlier. These wild price fluctuations have created what blogger Joe Costello has called the *oil yoke*, which threatens to hold back the global economy for years to come.[26] As the economy strives to recover, demand for oil increases; but because production can no longer keep up with demand, the price of oil surges, and this surge in price acts as a yoke, dragging the economy back into recession. Repeat ad infinitum, unless you can figure out how to throw off the yoke.

But in America, as in much of the rest of the developed world, the political discussion isn't about how to throw off the yoke; instead, our political discussion focuses on how to make the yoke more comfortable, or to pretend it isn't there. On one side of the political aisle, lip service is paid to investing in alternative energy sources. But oil is not just another energy source; oil is the foundation of our global economy. Solar panels can't make plastics or fertilizer; nor are wind turbines very efficient at flying Kiwis from New Zealand to New Hope, Michigan. On the other side of the aisle, we hear calls for increased production of domestic crude oil, the development of alternative fuels such as tar sands and oil shale, and squeezing more oil from existing fields (where only about 40 percent of available oil is recovered) through such techniques as "hydrofracking," or hydraulic fracturing.

Yet such chants of "Drill, Baby, Drill!" are no more than wishful thinking. The chant might be catchy, but it fails to address how increasing domestic production and using up our national resources more quickly leads to greater energy security—though one supposes the logic follows the same line of thinking as eating up one's seed corn to assuage the pangs of hunger. For example, the *proven* oil reserves in the United States in 2010 were about twenty-nine billion barrels, according to the US Energy Information Administration. That sounds like a lot, but for a nation that consumes 7.3 billion barrels annually, that represents just four years of supply, if we were able to pluck all that oil out of the ground in one fell swoop and use only domestic oil. (The actual reserves-to-production ratio—the rate at which we could get oil out of the ground—is just over eleven years.[27]) Nearly every day, of course, one can read about discoveries of "major" new fields of oil or tar sands, but these "major" discoveries are Lilliputian when compared to the gargantuan appetite of the global economy. Consider the "vast reserves" of the Bakken formation, beneath Montana, North Dakota, and Saskatchewan, which contains up to 24 billion barrels of oil, or the "major reserves" of perhaps 20 billion barrels in the Gulf of Mexico. Then do the math: the world uses 80 million barrels of oil per day, or just over 29 billion barrels *per year*.

Understanding the concept of energy returned on energy invested (EROEI) makes even more clear the speciousness of the notion that we can continue to drill our way to prosperity. The idea of EROEI is a simple one: divide the amount of energy you receive from a source by the amount of energy you expend retrieving it, and you'll have a sense of how productive or useful that energy source is. The sweet, easy-to-get crude oil pumped out of the ground in the 1970s, for example, had an EROEI of 30 to 1, which means for every unit of energy you put into extracting it, you received 30 units of energy—a massive surplus that has allowed the world to build roads, factories, jetliners, and a globalized economy fueled by cheap credit and cheap energy. (Before 1930, when it virtually bubbled out of the ground in certain locales, oil had an EROEI of 100 to 1.) Currently, the EROEI on most domestic crude oil is about 15 to 1: it takes twice as much energy to retrieve conventional crude today as it did forty years ago, because the easy stuff is now gone. These rates of energy returned on energy invested plummet precipitously when one looks toward the "Saudi Arabias" of oil shale and tar sands supposedly contained beneath such places as the Green River formation of Wyoming, Colorado, and Utah, or when one looks at the efficiency of biofuels. Tar sands and oil shale have an EROEI of barely 5, while corn ethanol has an EROEI of just 3.[28]

The effect of EROEI on our ability to run our economy on alternative sources of energy is the same effect that interest rates have on a retiree's ability to survive on an annuity. With an EROEI of 15, we are able to run a globalized economy with 3,000-mile supply chains and drive whichever large vehicle we desire, just as a retiree with a $1,000,000 annuity paying 15 percent can live quite comfortably on the coast of Florida, with trips to Europe and the Caribbean in between. But when that interest rate plummets to 5 percent, suddenly that same retiree is living in the house he grew up in Iowa, and a trip to the mall in Sioux City is a once-a-year luxury.

The political theater surrounding our energy policy ignores what geologists and the oil industry itself have been telling us for more than half a decade: that "the era of easy oil," as one global marketing campaign by Chevron put it as far back as 2005, is "over." Or, as the CEO of Total stated in 2007, "We have all been too optimistic about the geology." Or as Shell CEO Jeroen van der Veer wrote in 2008, "After 2015 supplies of easy-to-access oil and gas will no longer keep up with demand."[29] Yet political theater aside, the true debate about peak oil has become a question of effects and timing: few in the oil and gas industry argue with its basic premise.[30] Some maintain that the peak still lies in the future, with the most optimistic projections putting the date of global peak at 2020. The US military believes that "surplus oil production capacity could entirely disappear" by 2012.[31] Others argue that the date is already behind us; the International Energy Agency believes the peak in oil production happened in 2006.

But this focus on the *moment* when peak oil arrives—and whether that moment will be apocalyptic or merely the moment when the market begins to invest more aggressively in alternative energy sources—ignores the pressing reality of the *trend*. Peak oil won't put us back to the Stone Age. The average American uses twice as much energy as the average European, for example, to live at a relatively equal level of comfort;[32] thus the ability for Americans to maintain a high standard of living for some time through simple conservation is quite high. But the reality that the political theater and wishful thinking ignore is that we now live, or will soon live, in a world in which demand for energy outpaces supply—a fact that forces us to confront the very basis of our economic system and our belief that progress can be achieved only through growth.

TOO MANY, NOT ENOUGH

Talking about global peak oil or climate change through the rhetoric of apocalypse may make for good television and attention-grabbing editorials, but such apocalyptic framing hasn't mobilized the world into action. Instead, both peak oil and climate change have taken on the appearance and characteristics of partisan opinion, rather than of scientific evidence. Once entangled with the apocalyptic storyline, we doubt and debate the science behind both, or we claim forthwith not to "believe" in either. Perhaps the optimists are right, and technology will find new ways to replace crude oil production with synthetic oils or through increased extraction of oil shale and tar sands. And perhaps the global-warming deniers are right, and the melting ice caps have more to do with solar flares than with the more than eight hundred million cars and light trucks sputtering around the planet. While some react to the apocalyptic rhetoric of peak oil and global warming with denial and disbelief, the true believers spend their time in anticipation of future clarity (or future collapse). Yet neither the detractors nor believers are responding to the trends of global warming and peak oil realistically; rather they are seeing these trends through a distorted apocalyptic envisioning of them as events. And while busily arguing whether or not the world is ending by these two horsemen, we ignore the underlying trend that is propelling both global warming and peak oil: the exponential growth of human population and the strain that population is placing on the earth's resources and ecosystems.

The world population today is just over seven billion people—and there's another billion people who, if current trends continue, will be joining us in the next fifteen years. It's worth taking a moment to put that number into perspective. Twelve thousand years ago, at the dawn of agriculture, the number of humans on earth is estimated to have totaled fewer than ten *million* people—or just slightly more than the current population of New York City. Agriculture and then the rise of civilization enabled the human population to grow, but that rate of growth was relatively slow and stable, producing modest population growth from a modern perspective. When Jesus Christ was born to save humankind, for example, humankind was but three hundred million people, or about the total population of the United States today. It took from the time of Christ to the first settling of America by Europeans, or nearly 1,700 years, for that population to double. The "shot heard round the world" was heard by no more than 850 million people, and it wasn't until 1805, by most estimates, that the global human population first reached one billion.

Seen on a graph that plots population over time, the growth of humanity is a long, nearly flat line that extends across the horizontal axis for seemingly forever, and then suddenly hockey-sticks up into a near vertical rise—a rise that towers over the rest of history like an exclamation point. While it took more than 99 percent of all human history—more than 150,000 years—for the human population to reach the first one billion mark, the Industrial Revolution (and, with it, the capacity of humankind to use cheaper and more powerful types of energy in the form of steam and coal) allowed humanity to add the next billion people in just 128 years, reaching two billion by 1927. It was the 1920s, broadly speaking, that marked the beginning of the age of oil (and the age of the automobile), and it was that super-efficient form of energy, more powerful and more portable than coal or wood-fired steam, that allowed the growth of human population to accelerate at a rate previously unimaginable. Since 1961, when the human population reached three billion, it has taken a mere twelve or thirteen years for humanity to add the next billion people, with world population reaching four billion in 1974, five billion in 1987, six billion in 1999, and seven billion in 2011.[33]

While anyone born after 1961 is accustomed to the world growing by another billion roughly every decade, such growth was unthinkable less than a century ago. One needn't cite figures or charts as evidence that our population has surged in the twentieth century, for most Americans alive today have witnessed the effects of this staggering rate of population growth with our own eyes. We've seen it in the quiet childhood roads now gridlocked with traffic; the woods where we played cut down to make way for tract houses; the landscapes of our individual memories transformed by bricks, mortar, and pavement into a nearly endless chain of strip malls.

This pace of change and transformation is an exclusively modern phenomenon—and it is a pace of growth that appears to be butting firmly against the limits of the world's resources. In 2005, for example, with the global population just over six billion, we were already consuming resources 1.3 times as fast as the earth could renew them. If that figure seems abstract, just take a look at your grocery bill to understand what this means. In seven of the first eight years of the Apocalyptic Decade—for the first time in modern history—global demand for grains consistently out-stripped global supply. This surging demand for more grains has been driven not just by simple population growth but by the increasing wealth of developing nations, whose desire to emulate the American lifestyle often extends to the American diet of grain-intensive beef and poultry. Demand is also being driven—quite lit-erally, in this case—by the bipartisan push to turn more of the world's crops into ethanol to fuel our cars and trucks: in 2009, a full quarter of America's grain harvest was diverted to the production of biofuels.[34] The result of this increased demand for grains, whether to serve hamburgers in Beijing or to pump ethanol in Boston, has been apparent on any American grocery store shelf, where food prices in recent years have risen at a rate of more than 6.5 percent per year. Soaring demand has also resulted in a drawing down of the total stockpile of global grains, from a 115-day supply in 1990 to just 75 days in 2010. This shortage of grains and basic foodstuffs is already causing political unrest around the globe. The instability that swept across the Middle East in 2011, for example, was fueled in large part by soaring food prices; in Algeria, the crowds that braved the government's bullets on the streets of Algiers weren't just demanding democracy—they were demanding sugar.[35]

In the oceans, things are hardly any better. The global fish catch peaked in 1997 and has been declining ever since, with more than 20 percent of the world's fisheries on the verge of the type of cataclysmic collapse that wiped out nearly the entire cod industry in Newfoundland, Canada, in 1992.[36] Since 1998, more than a third of the world's ocean fisheries have faced a similar collapse. If current fishing trends continue, some see a complete global collapse of fisheries by the middle of this century.[37]

Care for a drink of water? Nearly 50 percent of the freshwater available on our planet has already been appropriated for human use—a figure that could rise to include nearly all the earth's available freshwater by the middle of this century, if current population and economic growth trends continue.[38] Yet even as demand for water increases, the global supply is increasingly threatened by climate change or damaged by runoff from fertilizers and industrial pollution—including the dramatically rising use of water to recover additional natural gas and oil through hydrofracking. Thus water—like oil, coal, timber, fisheries, productive farmland, and basic industrial minerals and elements from copper to helium—seems destined to enter a "peak" scenario, in which demand permanently exceeds supply if current trends continue.

To relieve the pressure of human overpopulation on the biosphere, economists and politicians often advocate raising the standard of living in developing nations to reduce the birthrate. But raising the standard of living to slow the rate of population growth is like smoking more cigarettes in the hope that their toxicity will kill the cancer cells in your lungs. Here's why: if we were to raise the standard of living in other countries to the extent that everyone lived an American lifestyle, we would require not two, not three, but five additional Earths, according to one study.[39] Consider the ecological impact of the American way of life. Representing just 5 percent of the world's population, we use 25 percent of the world's oil output every year—and, consequently, we emit one-quarter of the world's carbon dioxide and greenhouse gases. On average, we Americans flush and shower through three times more water than the average resident of Planet Earth. Each year, we consume nearly 300 pounds of meat per person, compared to 158 pounds for a European, and 60 pounds for a resident of a developing country.[40] Despite a decline in average household size from 3.1 people per household in 1970 to 2.6 in the year 2000, the average size of a new single-family home in America has increased from 1,400 square feet in 1970 to more than 2,300 square feet today.[41] There might be fewer of us in each household, but we consume and discard an ever-increasing amount of stuff. Out of each of those households we toss an average of five pounds of trash *every day*—more than five times the trash that people discard in even the most litter-strewn third-world nation.[42] Efforts to get Americans to recycle, to use less, and to gaze tree-ward on Earth Day have not succeeded in reversing the rising tide of resource consumption in the United States; while our population has doubled since 1960, our total resource consumption has tripled. In the last twenty years alone—two decades that have seen the introduction in America of compact fluorescent bulbs, hybrid cars, municipal recycling, and yoga—the American ecological footprint has increased by 20 percent.[43]

The gulf between the resources consumed by Americans (and not to single us out—the industrialized European and Asian lifestyles are less voracious only by a matter of degree) and the poorest nations is even more sobering. The world's richest 20 percent of people—which, if you are reading this book, undoubtedly includes you—consume 86 percent of the earth's total annual resources; the poorest 20 percent use a mere 1.6 percent. Those of us in the top fifth chow down 45 percent of all the world's meat and fish each year, while the poorest 20 percent scramble for 5 percent of the scraps. We burn through 58 percent of the world's energy—whether oil, natural gas, coal, nuclear, or renewable—

while the poorest fifth use less than 4 percent. We use 84 percent of the world's paper, compared to the poorest, who use barely more than 1 percent. And we own 84 percent of the vehicles and 74 percent of the world's telephone lines, compared to 1 and 1.5 percent, respectively, for the world's poorest fifth.[44]

The notion that we can solve these inequalities by raising the standard of living in developing countries without reducing our own, in a world already stretched beyond ecological capacity, is pure fantasy. Far from a tide that will "lift all boats" by raising the standard of living in third-world countries, globalization is more like a wave that is likely to crash much of humanity onto the rocks of a finite world.

The quickest way to alleviate the pressures of overpopulation is to reduce the consumption of the world's richest 20 percent. But as former president Jimmy Carter will tell you, that's not an argument that any American politician seeking election or reelection can make.

THE BATTLE FOR RESOURCES

Central to the argument that the world's soaring human population could soon imperil us are the ecological concepts of *carrying capacity* and *overshoot*. Carrying capacity is the maximum population of a particular species that a given environment can support without detrimental effects on that environment. Overshoot is the theory that, because of delayed feedback in the environment, a population can temporarily exceed its carrying capacity. Overshoot, ecologically, is *always* followed by a crash in the species' total population.[45]

A favorite example among ecologists of the consequences of overshoot are the reindeer of St. Matthew Island. In 1944, at the height of the Second World War, the US Coast Guard opened a station on this remote island in the Bering Sea and introduced a herd of twenty-nine reindeer to serve as a secondary food source for the small contingent of Coast Guardsmen stationed there. A little over a year later, with the end of World War II, the Coast Guard station was closed and the island abandoned. The reindeer, facing no natural predators on the 128-square-mile island blanketed with rich nutritious lichen, thrived; by 1957, the original herd of 29 reindeer had boomed to more than 1,350; by 1963, the herd had reached a peak of more than 6,000. Yet just three years later, in the summer of 1966, biologists returned to St. Matthew to study the herd, only to find a denuded landscape of sparse grasses and sedge strewn with thousands upon thousands of bones. Only forty-two of the reindeer had survived a nearly complete collapse of the herd during the previous winter. The reindeer population never recovered, and by 1980 the last remaining reindeer of St. Matthew had died off.[46]

The reindeer of St. Matthew make a classic example of carrying capacity, overshoot, and crash in part because their story is a simple one: a herd of reindeer, facing no natural predators, eat the landscape bare until there is nothing left to eat. Unable to migrate to more fertile grazing grounds because of the vast ocean that surrounds them, the population crashes.

Humans, of course, have a far more complex relationship with their environment. The capacity to increase the supply of food is available to us through resource management and the inputs of energy and technology. When that fails? Unlike the reindeer of St. Matthew, we have weapons; if there are too many people and not enough resources, humans will fight to gain control of what's left.

Conflicts over access to natural resources are the oldest form of human warfare, dating back before civilization and agriculture to a time when one prehistoric band of humans first decided to attack another to gain access to prime hunting grounds. These first skirmishes over control of resources grew in intensity and frequency with the rise of agriculture and civilization 12,000 years ago; eventually, as growing populations exhausted the local resources that had initially provided their rise to civilization, the new city-states into which people had organized themselves turned to expansionist policies and military conquest to maintain their new way of life, giving rise to the first empires.

Down through every era and age in history since then, from the Crusades (a five-century dispute over trade routes) to the nineteenth-century "Scramble for Africa" by European powers (whose new industrial factories had an insatiable appetite for raw resources) to Hitler's call for *Lebensraum* or Japan's expansion into Manchuria, the motivation for most of the world's military history is best understood as a competition for land, timber, minerals, trade routes, and sources of energy (such as slaves, coal, or—today—oil.)

But two important factors have given resource wars a new characteristic in the twenty-first century—and these factors virtually guarantee that resource conflicts will continue to embroil the world in the decades ahead. The first is the extent to which the competition for resources has entered an end-game period as peak oil, global population growth, climate change, and the growing appetites of the global economy combine to create a world in which demand for resources is permanently exceeding supply. We aren't just fighting for control of resources in a region anymore; we are fighting for the last of the goods in the whole world. The second is the degree to which we live in a world where gaining access to weapons has rarely been easier.

Increasingly, the United States has been willing to use its military might to secure access to vital resources, which, though it's considered gauche to mention in polite company, has been the primary strategic objective of America's military and foreign policy since becoming codified by President Jimmy Carter in 1980. As Andrew J. Bacevich—a professor of international affairs at Boston University, West Point graduate, and retired career army officer—has pointed out, the increased willingness to use our military came *after* the Cold War ended and *prior* to the attacks of 9/11,[47] or about the time that Francis Fukuyama was wringing his hands in despair over the "End of History" while telling America's foreign policy intelligentsia that our new, post–Cold War national mission should be to "build up material wealth at an accelerated rate" by securing global resources.[48]

In the more than forty years between 1945 and 1988, as Bacevich notes, "large-scale US military actions abroad totaled a scant six," yet in the less than fifteen years between the fall of the Berlin Wall in 1989 and the invasion of Iraq in 2003, the United States embarked on "nine major military interventions. . . . And that count does not include innumerable lesser actions such as Bill Clinton's signature cruise-missile attacks against obscure targets in obscure places, the almost daily bombing of Iraq throughout the late 1990s, or the quasi-combat missions that have seen GIs dispatched to Rwanda, Colombia, East Timor, and the Philippines."[49] With the fall of the Soviet Union, which had served as a countervailing force and a complicating consequence to the use of American military power for four decades, both political parties have pushed the boundaries of American interventionism. As President Bill Clinton's secretary of state Madeleine Albright famously and impatiently demanded of Colin Powell, "What's the point of having this superb military that you're always talking about, if we can't use it?"[50]

But we can use our military, and we increasingly are, and nowhere is this more evident than in the global struggle for oil and the proxy wars in Iraq, Afghanistan, and Libya to ensure the free flow of Middle Eastern oil to the global economy. The national press and protectors of political discourse in America reject as conspiracy the notion that our foreign policy is guided by the need for oil. Even former chairman of the Federal Reserve Alan Greenspan, the vaunted defender of globalization and free markets, was widely chastised by pundits when he wrote in his memoir that "it is politically inconvenient to acknowledge what everyone knows: the Iraq war is largely about oil."[51] But stating that American foreign policy is driven by the need to secure access to (though not necessarily direct control over) the world's oil and natural gas supplies is not a conspiracy; every president since Franklin Delano Roosevelt has publicly stated that access to oil is of vital national interest to the United States. Perhaps worse than this unwillingness to openly discuss what is apparent simply by looking at a map—for nearly wherever one finds oil, one will find an American military presence—is the misguided notion held by many well-meaning Americans that, if the wars in Iraq and Afghanistan are "largely about oil," as author and critic James Howard Kunstler has pointed out, then they are somehow "optional, a mistake, an indulgence, something we should not dirty our hands in."[52] But they are not optional, as long as Americans insist that access to cheap oil is our God-given right.

But as with the notion that we can halt population growth and the overuse of resources by raising the standard of living around the world, or the notion that we can reduce our dependence on fossil fuels by drilling them faster, the use of America's military resources to protect the world's oil supplies follows a circuitous logic. Oil, after all, is sold on the international market. Using American might to keep the oil flowing simply keeps it flowing to the international markets, while the declining value of the dollar that inevitably results from the debt burden of our military excursions ensures that the price of oil continues to rise.[53]

Meanwhile, the United States exacerbates the need for military adventures to secure global resources by arming the other side. Just as the United States spends roughly half the total world military expenditures on its own defense, it exports nearly half of all the world's arms every year. These weapons—from small arms and rocket launchers to tanks and aircraft—are ubiquitous in every corner of the globe; in 1999, weapons of US origin were being used in more than 92 percent of the conflicts under way around the world. This export of American armaments is hardly confined to democracies; in 2003, twenty of the top twenty-five US arms clients "were either undemocratic regimes or governments with records of major human rights abuses," according to the World Policy Institute.[54] Although the export of large, advanced weapons systems (including, naturally, nuclear material) is heavily regulated by the United States, the export of small arms—automatic rifles, machine guns, and grenades—is governed primarily by the profit motive. And profitable it is: the legal trade in small arms and light weapons is estimated to be between $7 billion and $10 billion per year, with perhaps an additional $2 billion to $3 billion a year traded through black-market channels. With an individual assault rifle on the global market costing less than $500, that's a lot of weapons making their way into conflicts around the world. Combined with long-simmering ethnic and racial tensions throughout the world and increasing pressure from overpopulation and resource depletion, this easy global access to guns has yielded predictable results: the number of armed conflicts has doubled from previous decades, with more than one hundred conflicts erupting across the globe since the end of the Cold War[55]—a trend in increased violence that is likely to continue in coming years.

APOCALYPTIC CONFUSION

Most of us are familiar with the platitude "When the only tool you have is a hammer, everything looks like a nail." In a similar way, our overreliance on the apocalyptic storyline stands between us and our ability to properly assess the problems before us. Some see the looming crises of global warming and resource and energy depletion and conclude that inaction will bring about the end of civilization: only through a radical shift toward clean energy and conservation, those on the Left argue, can we continue the way of life that we have known. Those on the Right dismiss the apocalyptic threats altogether, because the proposed solutions to peak oil, global warming, and overpopulation conflict with core conservative beliefs about deregulation and the free-market economy, or with a religious worldview that believes humanity is not powerful enough to alter something as large as our climate. Still others dismiss the catalog of doom and gloom as mere apocalypticism itself. Surely, we convince ourselves, all the dire warnings about the effects of global warming aren't that different from the world-ending expectations of the Rapturists?

The result is that the energy we could expend addressing the problems before us is instead consumed by our efforts to either dismiss the threat of apocalypse or to prove it real. Even the most ardent of believers in global peak oil and climate change spend more time trying to convince others that our fears are justified than trying to figure out how to address the problems we must confront. Ultimately, the question becomes not what to do about the threats before us but whether you *believe* in the threats before us.

By allowing the challenges of the twenty-first century to be hijacked by the apocalyptic storyline, we find ourselves awaiting a moment of clarity when the problems we must confront will become apparent to all—or when those challenges will magically disappear, like other failed prophecies about the end of the world. Yet the real challenges we must face are not future events that we imagine or dismiss through apocalyptic scenarios of collapse— they are existing trends. The evidence suggests that much of what we fear in the future—the collapse of the economy, the arrival of peak oil and global warming and resource wars—has already begun. We can wait forever, while the world unravels before our very eyes, for an apocalypse that won't come.

The rise of apocalyptic expectation in America suggests that the true question we face is not merely a matter of personal belief. The ultimate question we face may come disguised as arguments over conservation versus technological innovation, as military con- flicts over foreign oil versus promises of domestic energy indepen- dence, as debates over immigration versus humanitarian goodwill, or between the creation of jobs and the preservation of the envi- ronment. But the rise of apocalyptic expectation suggests that we face a deeper crisis, a crisis at the core of how we view the world. Despite the political bickering, Americans on both the Left and the Right share some fundamental beliefs about the world. What if those underlying beliefs no longer correspond with reality?

CHAPTER 6

IN DEFENSE OF A WORLDVIEW

Faced with the choice between changing one's mind and proving there is no need to do so, almost everyone gets busy on the proof.

—John Kenneth Galbraith,
A Contemporary Guide to Economics,
***Peace, and Laughter* (1971)**

Every generation of historians since Herodotus has labored to explain the problem that failed civilizations pose to the progressive ideal of history. Following Herodotus's example, many have focused on dramatic narrative explanations for the collapse of ancient societies. This is the (often grotesquely simplified) genre of history that most of us remember from school, in which the Roman Empire declines because Hannibal brought a bunch of elephants over the Alps, or in which Germany invades Poland because Hitler was rejected from art school. Occasionally, nature makes an appearance in this genre—it's hard to ignore the volcano at Pompeii, after all—but with the exception of such periodic cataclysms, the disappearance of most ancient civilizations has traditionally been explained through stories of coups and conquest.

In the late twentieth century, however, historians such as Clive

Ponting and Jared Diamond began incorporating scientific find-ings in the fields of environmental studies and paleoclimatology to answer the question of what happened to past, failed civilizations. Forgoing the traditional historian's bias of favoring dramatic nar-ratives to explain the problem of lost civilizations, their work has instead focused on more prosaic influences, such as soil erosion and resource depletion, to explain the failure of ancient societies.[1]

This new focus on environmental degradation as explanation for societal collapse has not been without controversy. It is diffi-cult, after all, to accept that the same societies that deciphered the circuitous motions of planets or that created complex alphabets and advanced mathematics to track the accounting of commerce would have failed to notice the erosion of their own crop fields or failed to communicate that erosion to important decision makers. The archaeologist Joseph Tainter argues that "one supposition of this view [that environmental destruction has caused societal col-lapse] must be that societies *sit by and watch the encroaching weak-ness without taking corrective actions.*"[2] Like many historians before him, Tainter rejects out of hand the notion that the decision makers of centralized, complex ancient societies would choose "idleness in the face of disaster."[3] Surely, when faced with the cata-clysmic threat of soil depletion and crop failure and starvation—or peak oil and global warming—people will choose to alter their belief systems, if only to ensure their own survival?

But, alas, they do not—or did not. Why, throughout history, have many civilizations failed to avert the mortal crisis they faced, ulti-mately leading to their destruction? Were they too primitive to observe the crisis before them? No; ignorance fails prima facie as an excuse for the collapse of many ancient societies, given their advances in mathematics, astronomy, and other scientific fields. Instead, many ancient societies failed for this simple reason: the changes societies needed to make to avert the crisis before them were antithetical to their accepted beliefs and customs;[4] their very *worldview* prevented them from making the necessary changes to avert disaster.

One example of this continued adherence to customs and beliefs in the face of environmental degradation can be found in the history of the Rapanui people on Easter Island. By the thirteenth century CE, the various clans of the Rapanui people had developed a complex cultural interaction in which each clan sought to one-up the others through the construction of ever-greater *moai*—the eerie sentinel rock figures for which Easter Island is famous. Though the construction of each rock figure consumed tremendous resources—not only through the quarrying of the stone from which they were carved but through the trees that were felled to form a sort of conveyor belt toward the *moai*'s eventual placement and raising—the Rapanui continued the tradition even as Easter Island became visibly denuded of forest around them. The Rapanui chose to pursue cultural enrichment over physical survival, and eventually the island was stripped of its primary, protective vegetation. With their crops now unprotected from the merciless Pacific winds, the Rapanui were plunged into centuries of impoverishment and hunger.[5]

Such cultural obstinance is put in even starker relief when one compares the fates of the Inuit people and the Norse settlers of Greenland.

In 984 CE, Erik the Red—the archetypical Viking whose violent run-ins with his neighbors are chronicled in the Icelandic sagas—returned home after a three-year banishment from Iceland with tales of a rugged, beautiful, and entirely uninhabited island just a few days' sailing to the west. Erik the Red wasn't the first Icelander to set eyes on the imposing, ice-choked coast of the world's largest island, but he was arguably the first to see its potential; during his years of banishment, he had sailed around the southern tip of the island and up the western coast, where he discovered two deep, ice-free fjords whose surrounding terraced hillsides appeared suitable for farming and settlement. Famously, on his return to his native land, he named the entire island "Greenland"—a selective, if not downright misleading, moniker that overlooked the massive ice cap covering more than 80 percent of the island—to attract potential settlers. Soon Erik the Red had assembled a fleet of twenty-five ships and filled them with Icelanders who were eager to pay the small fee for passage in exchange for the promise of a new life in the green lands to the west. In 986, they departed for Greenland and established two settlements near the deep fjords on the western coast—the first permanent European settlements of North America.

The Norse weren't the first humans to settle in Greenland, of course; Paleo-Eskimos had sporadically inhabited the island beginning as early as 2500 BCE, following the caribou herds and whale pods from Labrador and the Arctic during periods in which global temperatures were warm enough to make human survival in Greenland a possibility. But such "warmer" periods were relative; over a period of nearly three thousand years, the return of plunging temperatures forced the Paleo-Eskimos to abandon Greenland multiple times. And in all likelihood, Greenland was again uninhabited when the first settlers arrived with Erik the Red in 986.[6]

Just as when they had settled Iceland a century before, the Vikings brought to Greenland an agrarian way of life that had allowed them to become wealthy in temperate Northern Europe, but it would soon prove inuring when practiced on the fragile soils and in the unforgiving arctic climate of Greenland. For example, the terraced hillsides above the fjords where the Vikings settled were quickly converted to pastureland and hayfields for the cattle, pigs, and sheep that the Vikings had brought with them. But the pigs and sheep steadily nibbled Greenland's native willows and birches to near-nothingness, and without the protection from the cold Arctic wind provided by the willow and birch, growing hay in the fields became more and more difficult. With each passing decade, yields from the summers' harvests steadily dropped; eventually the settlers would find themselves force-feeding seaweed to their prized cows in the hopes that they would survive the lengthening, dark Greenland winters.

Yet those hardships, and the full impact of depleting resources on the settlers' hopes for survival, would come later; initially, the Viking settlers at Greenland prospered. Tales of success brought more settlers in the wake of the first pioneers; eventually, nearly five thousand Norse would occupy the two settlements first established by Erik the Red's fleet. In addition to harvesting hay for their livestock, the settlers learned to hunt seal and caribou and cultivated small gardens of cabbage, beets, and lettuce for themselves. From Norway they imported iron, timber, and tar (to preserve wood) while exporting walrus skins and tusks and live polar bears and gyrfalcons, which were viewed as worldly status symbols in medieval Europe. The settlers also imported their devoutly European and Christian identity. Despite their distance as "Europe's most remote outpost,"[7] they regularly tithed to the Catholic Church, built a series of parish churches and a cathedral replete with an imported brass bell and stained-glass windows, and slavishly followed the latest fashions from Norway. They considered themselves to be Europeans, rather than Greenlanders—a self-image that would soon have profound consequences.

Although they didn't know it, the fact that the Norse settlers were able to succeed at all in Greenland was made possible by a bit of fortuitous climatic luck. Beginning in the early years of the tenth century, the North Atlantic region had entered another period of warming—known today as the Medieval Warm Period —which would last (less fortuitously, for the Norse in Greenland) until the beginning of the fourteenth century.

These warming temperatures also brought Native Americans back to Greenland. Beginning around 1200 CE, the Norse began to encounter a group of people to the north who were following the caribou herds through their summer migrations. The Norse called these people *skraelings*, or wretches; being slightly more politically correct than Vikings (at least occasionally), we know that the hunters following the caribou across Greenland were actually the Inuit people, who crossed the Bering Strait from the Canadian Arctic and into Greenland during the Medieval Warm Period.[8]

We also know that within 250 years of the Inuit's arrival, the Norse settlements had disappeared entirely from Greenland. And thus we are again faced with that oldest and most basic of the historian's problems: the problem of the disappeared. What happened to them?

Not long after the Inuit arrived in Greenland, the climate shifted again: the Medieval Warm Period came to an end, and a period of dramatic cooling—known as the Little Ice Age—began. By the beginning of the fourteenth century, temperatures in the Northern Hemisphere had begun to drop precipitously. In Northern Europe, cooler summers and colder springs caused a series of crop failures, resulting in the persistent, recurring famines that devastated Europe's population throughout the fourteenth century. In Greenland, the Little Ice Age proved disastrous to the

Norse's hayfields and their pastoral way of life, eventually leading to mass starvation and the disappearance of the Norse settlements by the early 1400s.

Yet to claim that the Norse disappeared because of the catastrophe of plunging global temperatures is to ignore one critically important caveat: long after the Norse outposts vanished, the Inuit remained in an ever-colder Greenland. The Little Ice Age didn't make it impossible for humans to survive in Greenland for the half a millennium during which the cooling period persisted (it ended, rather abruptly, in the middle of the nineteenth century). So why did the Norse disappear?

The answer can be found in their allegiance to their cultural worldview. The Norse Greenlanders could see that the Inuit were continuing to thrive in the unrelenting cold, even as their own settlements withered and their crops failed in the shorter growing season. The example of how to survive in the declining temperatures was right before them, for "the Inuit represented the climax of thousands of years of cultural developments by Arctic peoples learning to master Arctic conditions."[9] While the Norse shivered all winter long in cold earthen houses with little wood to heat them, the Inuit survived comfortably in igloos warmed by whale and seal blubber. When the caribou, seals, and walruses that supplemented the Norse diet disappeared from the increasingly ice-choked shoreline, the Inuit kept themselves well fed by chasing seals and whales into the open waters of the North Atlantic with their harpoons and kayaks. Yet the Norse, even at their most emaciated end, never copied the Inuit's example or adopted their technologies, even though the success of the Inuit in adapting to the plunging temperatures was plainly visible to them.

In part, the Norse failed to copy the Inuit's ways because they considered the Inuit an inferior people—they were *skraelings*, after all: wretches. Yet even without the cultural adaptations of the Inuit, the Norse could have survived the increasing cold by harvesting Greenland's most abundant resource: fish.

There was, however, one significant and ultimately insurmountable hurdle to this solution: the Norse settlers of Greenland didn't eat fish. Although their ancestors and contemporaries in Norway and Iceland had eaten fish, the early Greenland Norse settlers had developed a cultural taboo against the dietary practice. The pull of that taboo would prove stronger than the pangs of hunger. In a culture that glorified adherence to tradition, a solution to starvation that required giving up that tradition was truly unthinkable, and so the Greenland Norse in the final decades of their existence remained focused on shepherding and trade with Europe, clinging to their worldview and culinary taboos—even past the brink of their own starvation.[10] During their final dark and hungry winter, they turned to eating their last prized calves and then their dogs, but never the abundant fish that swam in thick schools in the fjords and coastal waters just outside the barns where they huddled and finally succumbed to starvation. "To them . . . concerned with their social survival as much as their biological survival," Diamond writes, "it was out of the question to invest less in churches, to imitate or intermarry with the Inuit, and thereby to face an eternity in Hell just in order to survive another winter on Earth."[11] It was equally out of the question to adopt the ways of the Inuit or to break their cultural taboo against eating fish. To the end, the Greenland Norse defended their worldview—and by 1450 they were gone.

"Civilizations die from suicide," wrote the great historian Arthur J. Toynbee, "Not from murder."[12]

The Inuit remain in Greenland to this day.

THE DENIAL OF DEATH AND THE END OF A WORLDVIEW

Science offers an explanation for why the Norse in Greenland— and other cultures throughout history—chose fealty to their beliefs over the chance for survival. Recent research in psychology tells us that when we're faced with danger, we're more likely to cling to our beliefs than to change them, and when our worldview is threatened, we are psychologically predisposed to cling ever more tightly to our beliefs.

In 1974, Ernest Becker, a cultural anthropologist at Syracuse University, won the Pulitzer Prize for his psychological and philosophical masterpiece *The Denial of Death*. The knowledge of our own mortality, Becker argues, "haunts the human animal like nothing else."[13] Others have made the same observation throughout the ages, but Becker added to this rather commonplace pronouncement a bold hypothesis: finding ways to deny our own mortality is the mainspring of most human activity. Escaping or at least alleviating the anxiety we feel over our own death is among our primary psychological motivators—and it is this need to "deny death" that compels human beings to create and embrace culture.

Faced with the awful knowledge that we are mortal in the physical world, Becker notes, human beings subconsciously seek to find immortality and solace in the symbolic world of culture—that is, through our values and beliefs. *I* may die as an individual, the artist or writer says, but I will live on through my work; death may come for *me*, the parent says, but part of me will live on in my children and their children; the soldier or patriot may die, but he or she will have died in the service of the nation's cause; the body of the religious faithful may expire, but their spirits will ascend to eternal life in heaven; and so on and so forth. The specific beliefs are irrelevant, because from a functional standpoint the secularist's belief in the institutions of democracy are no different from the evangelical's faith in God. Both serve, according to Becker, to place the mortal individual into the context of a larger, immortal story.[14]

It is only once that larger story is in place that an individual is able to reenact the heroic myth, which Becker believes is central to our self-identity and sense of purpose. The nun stays pious to be rewarded by God; the father provides and protects to earn the love and respect of his children and wife; even the uninspired office drone is solicitous to earn the approval of upper management. By replacing the existential terror of an indifferent universe with the ordered story of cultural beliefs, the individual is able to attain "a feeling of primary value," as Becker calls it: "of cosmic specialness, of ultimate usefulness to creation, *of unshakable meaning.*"[15]

Becker's thesis—that the primary purpose of culture is to mitigate our individual fear of death—represented one of the grandest reconsiderations of the role of death in psychology and culture since Sigmund Freud. By 1984, three graduate students in experimental social psychology at the University of Kansas—Sheldon Solomon, Jeff Greenberg, and Tom Pyszczynski—had distilled Becker's thesis into a formal theory they call *Terror Management Theory*. Terror Management Theory declares that "to maintain psychological equanimity throughout their lives, people must sustain . . . faith in a culturally derived worldview that imbues reality with order, stability, meaning and permanence; and . . . a belief that one is a significant contributor to this meaningful reality."[16]

Solomon and his colleagues created a series of experiments to determine the scientific validity of Terror Management Theory. If the purpose of our cultural worldviews is to reduce our psychological fear of death, the psychologists reasoned, then people, when reminded of death, would turn to their cultural worldviews for reassurance that human life does indeed have meaning and purpose. Even more so, they reasoned, people should in fact bolster and defend their belief systems when faced with reminders of death—a subconscious reaction to mortality that Solomon and his colleagues call *worldview defense.*

In their most famous experiment on worldview defense, Solomon and his colleagues reminded one group of Christian students of their mortality by showing them the gruesome film *Faces of Death.* Another group of Christian students, serving as a control group, was shown a lighthearted comedy. Both sets of students were then asked to evaluate essays written by Jewish and Christian students. The students who had experienced reminders of their own mortality were significantly more critical of the essays written by the Jewish students; their criticism at times bordered on the anti-Semitic. Just as worldview defense had predicted, the Christian students who had been reminded of death sought to bolster their own worldviews by denigrating the beliefs of others.

The display of worldview defense isn't limited to the religious. Other experiments showed that German students who have been reminded of their mortality will sit farther away from immigrant Turks than German students who have not received such a reminder; judges in Arizona whose mortality has been evoked are more likely to hand down harsher sentences; and so on and so forth. To date, more than three hundred experiments in fifteen countries have demonstrated that regardless of one's cultural or religious background, people, when reminded of death, will react negatively to those who threaten or differ from their worldview and will react more positively to those who uphold their worldview.[17]

Worldview defense provides a psychological explanation for why, when faced with calamity, people don't make the changes necessary to avert disaster: when faced with a mortal threat, we are more likely to cling to our cultural beliefs than to change them. It helps us to understand why the Norse settlers—who were painfully aware that they were starving to death as the cold of the Little Ice Age ravaged their crops on the terraced hillsides of Greenland— found it inconceivable to adopt the habits of the *skraelings* in order to adapt to the developing trend of colder temperatures. According to psychologists, worldview defense leads us to exhibit *in-group bias*—kindness toward those who are like us and antipathy toward those who are not. That antipathy toward the other, and fealty to their own, eventually caused the Norse in Greenland to disappear entirely from the face of the earth.

We can see this tendency to exhibit in-group bias in the apocalyptic fantasies that we conjure today. Central to all modern apocalyptic narratives is the need to feel morally and ethically on the side of right; apocalyptic stories prove our beliefs correct, while proving the beliefs of the "Other" as wrong. When it seems like nothing can continue as it is, the apocalyptic storyline assures us that the one thing that *will* continue is the rightness of our worldview.

Consider, for example, the environmentalist who harangues you with facts and figures about global warming, the loss of biodiversity, and the incredible waste produced by our industrial way of life. When the sea levels rise and global warming finally arrives, then everyone will understand—at last!—what the environmentalist already knows: that Bubba can't drive his clanking F350 with dually tires without repercussions, because it's the ecology, stupid. Or consider the fundamentalist Christian who tells you stories of the Rapture and the return of Christ, of Judgment Day, and of the coming

Kingdom of God. The details and timing may vary, but the point of the Rapture is to save the faithful while casting nonbelievers—usually gays, feminists, Democrats, and the aforementioned environmentalist—into eternal damnation. Or consider the libertarian goldbug who insists that when the Federal Reserve finishes papering over decades of bad debt with the printing press and when the dollar finally collapses as the world's reserve currency, we will be met with such hyperinflation—the Rapture as a form of sticker shock—that Americans will be cast down to a third-world standard of living, and the world will finally understand the dangers of fiat currencies and the importance of saving (in gold coins, of course).

Each of these apocalyptic fantasies follows a familiar pattern. Whether the gays are cast into hell or Bubba with his SUV finally understands the error of his ways, in every instance, the purpose of the anticipated apocalyptic moment is to *vindicate* one's beliefs. The apocalyptic moment resolves with finality the tensions between good and evil, between believer and nonbeliever, between environmentalist and capitalist—and the holder of the apocalyptic vision invariably comes out on top. In his imaginary future, the nature lover living on his sustainable compound will be proven correct—he will survive the cataclysm of environmental collapse because he is living in accord with Gaia. The fundamentalist who is Raptured up to heaven, or who remains to see the Kingdom of God on earth, will have her faith vindicated and will see paradise while nonbelievers suffer damnation. The financial bear with his buried loot of gold American Eagle coins will be secure while the rest of the world burns worthless American dollars for heat.

Such fantasies, however, are just that—fantasy. They belie the interconnectedness of the world and our shared fate. So why do we continue to turn to the apocalyptic fantasy?

For many years, anthropologists theorized that the apocalyptic imagination takes hold primarily in societies that are deprived or oppressed. Yet deprivation theory fails to explain the surge in apocalyptic thought across the political and spiritual spectrum in the richest and most powerful country in the world at the beginning of the twenty-first century. Worldview defense suggests that deprivation isn't the primary source of apocalyptic anxiety—doubt is.

It is the threat of losing one's cultural identity—not fears of personal mortality or mere deprivation—that elicits the apocalyptic impulse. It was not the loss of their kingdom to the Babylonians or, later, the Greeks, that caused the Jewish people to turn to visions of the apocalypse as a promise of salvation; rather, it was the threatened loss of their cultural cohesion (through the process of Hellenization) that they ultimately found intolerable, leading them to both rebellion and apocalyptic anticipation. So, too, did the earliest Christians cling to the apocalypse as a means of preserving, validating, and vindicating their beliefs and identity as they retreated to remote, scattered outposts in the face of brutal persecution by the Romans. Other outbreaks of apocalyptic anticipation follow a similar pattern. The Native American ghost dance (which borrowed elements from the Christian anticipation of a return of Christ and raising of the dead) emerged among the Paiute people and spread to other Native American tribes beginning in 1890—long after most tribes had lost their freedom and their land but at a point when they were in danger of losing their group identity, as Native children were forced into boarding schools and as young adults began to leave impoverished reservations in search of employment in cities and on farms.[18]

If the apocalyptic impulse can be understood as a form of cultural worldview defense, though writ on a larger and more global scale, then the ubiquity of apocalyptic anticipation in America today raises an important question: What is causing progressive environmentalists and libertarian goldbugs and conservative neo-cons to each embrace an apocalyptic vision of the future? The Christian expectation of the apocalypse is, of course, inseparable from Christian theology. But the turning of the secular mind toward an apocalyptic vision of the future—regardless of one's political persuasion—suggests not the end of the world but the end of our worldview.

A MAP WITHOUT A LEGEND BOX

A worldview is a set of assumptions and beliefs about the world held by an individual or group. The Belgian philosopher Leo Apostel imagined the concept of worldview "as a map that people use to orient and explain, and from which they evaluate and act, and put forward prognosis and visions of the future."[19] A world-view not only encompasses an explanation of the world but also answers this question: *Where are we going?*

For nearly five hundred years, since the beginning of the Enlightenment, the secular mind rarely hesitated when answering that question. The map of progress that we were following led us toward a more perfect world: a world perpetually improving through scientific discoveries; material growth; the accumulation of wealth; breakthroughs in technology; and advances in education, equality, and democracy. And for more than five hundred years, that map has proven nearly infallible—for it perfectly represented the world as it was. A still-young world and the virgin continents of the Americas lay waiting for humanity (or, at least, for the European mind) to establish dominion over them. The map led directly to the Americas, to the revolutions in the colonies and in France, to the colonization of Africa and the Far East by European powers, and to the unlocking of vast resources to fuel the new factories of industry that arose on both sides of the Atlantic. By the nineteenth century, the map showed the way westward in the United States; by the early twentieth century, it revealed the wonders of the age of oil. Advances in technology made it possible for us to speak instantly to anyone anywhere in the world and to travel to any place on the globe in less than a day. Like gods, we could conjure fruit from the tropics in the middle of a New England winter.

By the end of the twentieth century, when America emerged as the lone superpower in the post–Cold War world, the dream of raising the rest of the world to the same high standard of living that we had achieved became the bipartisan ideal of globalization. The map of progress had proven so accurate that much of the world was following it—the only way forward, we believed, was forward. This headlong rush toward globalization was unrelenting. In 1975, only 8 percent of countries worldwide had liberal free-market capitalist regimes; by 1997, 28 percent did.[20] Today, in the BRIC countries of Brazil, Russia, India, and China, a massive new middle class is emerging. India's middle class, to use but one example, is expected to grow 67 percent by 2016 to 267 million people, or nearly a quarter of India's population.[21]

Yet even as this new global middle class grows in both power and appetite, the specter of extreme poverty still haunts the world. After more than a quarter of a century of reducing trade barriers and opening up foreign markets, more than three billion people— nearly half the world's population—live on less than $2.50 per day, according to the World Bank.[22] Yet already, we have witnessed how

the accelerating consumption resulting from globalization has decimated the world's resources. What was once a critique leveled
solely by environmentalists has become increasingly self-evident to
many others: our belief in progress, in globalization and free markets and endless growth, is colliding with the limits of a finite world
and the edges of scientific achievement. This belief in continuous
growth is under grave doubt not just among foresighted environmentalists and naturalists but among the millions of Americans
who have seen their healthcare and energy costs soar while their
401(k)s have plunged, their wages have remained flat, and the
weather outside their windows has grown ever more strange. The
system that was supposed to lift us all out of poverty instead seems
poised to cast many of us into poverty.

Still, we can't quite give up the notion that continued economic growth, which we call progress, is the only way forward.
This belief in continued advancement is closely intertwined with
our cultural identity, in our belief in the American Dream and in
American exceptionalism. We really can't imagine what the point
of life would be if our work didn't produce material gains or if we
felt the future wouldn't be "better" than the past. We might dis-
agree on the way forward—on whether we should "Drill, Baby,
Drill!" or seek to build a more "sustainable" way of continuing to
live as we do now—but nearly all of us believe that our purpose
should be the pursuit of a continuously rising standard of living.
The worldview that we all share, regardless of political persuasion
or disagreements about the way forward, has been born from centuries of looking at that map.

And yet that map no longer reflects the world we live in. A
worldview based on endless material growth could be sustained in
a world of less than a billion people, with vast continents yet to be

exploited. In a world of seven billion people—with a burgeoning global middle class that is already living beyond resource limits—this belief in continued progress is disconnected from reality. The crisis we face is not just a crisis of climate or economy or growth or limited resources, or even a crisis of political and economic philosophy. Rather, what we are encountering is a metaphysical crisis. What we may be experiencing, at the edges of our vision and discourse, is not merely the possible end of the American century. Contained within the challenges of global warming, resource and energy depletion, and continued population growth lies the often unacknowledged, existential doubt over the idea of progress itself. The map no longer reflects the world; increasingly, the legend box has become indecipherable.

Worldview defense tells us that such moments of cultural doubt produce in the human animal a deep psychological terror. During such moments, our instinct is to cling more closely to our cultural beliefs—to our belief that unadulterated economic growth will return, that technology will solve global warming, and that human ingenuity will allow us to ameliorate the problem of human overpopulation. When such beliefs feel hollow—when it seems technology won't solve global warming or the energy crisis and that economic growth will not return—we turn to the apocalyptic storyline to explain the disconnect between reality and belief. Worldview defense may arise when we, as individuals, feel a mortal threat, but the rise of apocalyptic anxiety tells us that our worldview isn't merely under threat—it tells us that the foundations of that worldview have already begun to erode.

Our plight is not new: past societies have faced the problem of a worldview no longer reflecting observable reality. The work of Jared Diamond and others illustrates that when the cultural beliefs of a society no longer serve their intended role—to provide both meaning and a mode of behavior that ensures the survival and prosperity of the culture—adhering to the cultural worldview only hastens the threat. The Norse of Greenland clung to their image of themselves as Europeans and adhered to their cultural taboo against eating fish, even as their children and neighbors died of starvation; so, too, do we cling to our belief that continued economic growth is the only way forward, even as we witness the approaching ecological and resource limits to growth. Though the threats facing us are obvious and apparent, the solutions are hidden behind, or would undermine, our shared worldview.

It is precisely in such times of deep cultural contradiction that we would expect the apocalyptic archetype to become widespread—to leave the fringes of religious and paranoid thought and become a place of refuge for mainstream anxiety. And so we tell ourselves that we'll either develop the technologies to avert global warming, or all of life will cease to exist; we'll either turn to the gold standard and abolish fiat currency, or face complete economic collapse; we'll either find an alternative to oil through the development of hydrogen-powered cars and a clean energy economy, or we'll go back to the Stone Age.

History shows that when faced with such metaphysical crises, cultures either adapt their worldview to the new reality, or the society collapses. Worldview defense tells us that change doesn't come easy, if it comes at all: when the solutions required to solve a crisis are in opposition to a cultural worldview (as with the Norse), the culture finds itself headed for disaster. Even as the threat intensifies, worldview defense suggests that we'll cling more closely to the very worldview that is causing us harm. The outcome of such situations is purely binary: cultures either collapse when their worldview fails to adapt, or, alternately, the culture adapts, the world continues, and a new worldview evolves to reflect the actual circumstances facing the society. There is no other way out.

This is the pattern that we now find ourselves in, a feedback loop from which we must find a way to break free.

There is no small amount of irony in the fact that we are much more comfortable contemplating the total annihilation of civilization than entertaining the notion that how we view the world might be in need of some revision. But nonetheless, here we are. In these moments of doubt, when we question whether the map we've been following can still tell us the way forward, the apocalypse is the story we turn to for reassurance—for *meaning*—when our worldview no longer reflects the realities of the world we live in.

Yet to allow ourselves to be seduced by the story of apocalypse is like clutching the railing of a sinking ship. The solid feel of the familiar wood and metal may make you feel more secure, but to survive, you have to get off the ship.

CHAPTER 7

Beyond the Last Myth

At some point in our lives, many of us sense the impermanence of history. Something happens to expand our perspective to just the right historical focal point where we can perceive, for the first time, that the world that has seemed so permanent, so exemplary of the way things have always been, is itself but a recent and transient incarnation of human life. I remember a summer when I was eight years old, a summer spent with my grandparents at their house on a golf course in Sarasota, Florida. One night, as I sat in the cool air-conditioned confines of the den, exhausted after a day spent frolicking in my grandparents' pool, a film adaptation of Marjorie Rawlings's *Cross Creek* came on the television. In the film, Rawlings flees a bad marriage in New York and retreats to the swampy hinterlands of Florida during the first Florida land bubble in the 1920s, where she purchases a dilapidated cabin surrounded by a sprawling and weed-choked orange grove. She attempts to fix up the property while struggling to write a novel, interacting with a number of off-kilter and often alcoholic locals. The story itself shouldn't have been particularly mesmerizing to an eight-year-old boy. But the sense of place portrayed in the film was powerful; it felt as though the stifling, humid heat of the orange groves seeped through the television screen and into my grandparents' den.

Slowly the realization began to dawn on me that the Florida I knew—this Florida of newly built homes and jovial retirees and manicured golf courses and spotless macadam streets—was a recent invention, as transient and illusory as the orange glow that reflected in the golf course ponds when the sun set following an afternoon thundershower. I remember the next morning, sitting at the breakfast table and staring at my grandparents, feeling as though the very anchors of the permanent world had become unmoored. With childish conviction, I had assumed that grandparents had *always* retired to Florida; my own grandparents lived with such certitude, as though this house on the golf course had been their plan all along. But fifty years ago, this place had been an unlivable, fetid, backwater swamp. And what would it be like in sixty more years, when I retired? What else had I taken for granted as true and permanent and immutable, only to discover that its very existence was dependent on the steady hum of the rusting air conditioner, hung in the lightless window?

We know that we no longer live in the world of our grandparents, of course. We no longer trust that we can take a certain job and retire in twenty years with a pension in Florida—airconditioning or no. The solid framework of culture that once allowed us to dream that our children will grow up to take their own children on a motoring tour of the west to see the glaciers of Glacier National Park is no longer in place. And yet we hold fast to the belief that a stable middle class and continuous technological improvements are our birthright. This postwar vision of prosperity and stability, we tell ourselves, is the way things permanently ought to be: it is, after all, not just the American Dream but the "Amer-

ican way of life" that Dick Cheney famously declared as "not negotiable" just over a decade ago.[1] But the world has moved on, and it
is from the dissonance between the ideal and the reality—between
suburban motoring and global warming, for example, or between
middle-class optimism and the slowly tightening noose of a
declining paycheck, if one still has a paycheck—that our dreams of
apocalypse emerge. A clear and decisive end, a black-and-white
moment that defines us and our time, is preferable to a less con-
clusive, slow unraveling with no real saviors and victors.

Perhaps it is not the world we are in danger of losing but the
certainty of our place within it.

*   *   *

While there is no biological or psychological imperative in the
human animal for an expectation of an end to history—or even in
the *idea* of history—within the Judeo-Christian tradition there have
been generations of believers who have anticipated or longed for the
end of the world. Armed with the benefit of hindsight, we might dismiss these beliefs of our forbears as naive or antiquated—or with the
mild sense of (arrogant) pity that one sometimes feels when one con-
siders those poor souls who remain forever trapped within the
constraints of their historical era. The world, despite the expectations of those who came before us, quite clearly hasn't ended; our
very existence, generations later, stands as evidence that all expectations of apocalypse are ultimately fallacious and foolhardy.

But reason and evidence have never been able to fully dispel
our fear of ghosts, and we remain haunted by the ghosts of apocalypse, no matter how often we scoff at those in the past who have
believed the end would come within their lifetimes. Perhaps what

haunts us is the knowledge that for many who made those ancient prophesies—the Millerites of the nineteenth century, for example—*their* world, the world they knew, no longer exists. Nearly everything that they knew in the world, the sensual experiences that buttressed the meaning of their lives—the clop clop clop of horses delivering milk, the sound of music sung by a beloved cousin, the tumult of the markets where they wrangled over the price of this autumn's wheat—is now gone, erased forever by the tides of time. Were they to somehow come back today and stand on the very soil where they lived their entire lives, what would they recognize? Everything human they knew in the world has long since gone; the entire framework of culture on which they hung the meaning of their lives, the people they knew and loved and who gave their lives a singular richness, have long since disappeared. If the world itself hasn't ended, their world—as well as their worldview—long since has.

Worldviews are transient—far more changeable, in fact, than they may seem from our individual perspectives. Rome collapsed, but the Romans lived on among the ruins; over time they adapted their worldview to fit their new, changing circumstances. Their gods may have fled the Pantheon, but the world didn't end. Worldviews age and die like people; some die in a quick and sudden aneurism, a great, climactic upheaval; but most pass through the slow, dreary loss of teeth and hunching of backs until there is no doubt the decline has happened, but when precisely it happened, they can't say. Even language—the ultimate reflection of culture—changes so as to be nearly unrecognizable every five hundred years, linguists tell us.[2] Yet "there is no reason for amazement," as Robinson Jeffers wrote: "Surely one always knew that cultures decay, and life's end is death."[3]

The worldviews in which we embed our lives to give them greater meaning—whether that meaning comes from patriotism, art, family, or God—are themselves symbolic constructions that were created by human beings and validated by the joint consensus of other human beings. There is nothing else there; the world is no more or less than that. We can, therefore, create a new worldview. As Thomas Paine wrote, we have it in our power—yes, even within our power as mere individuals on a seemingly runaway planet teeming with more than seven billion people—to begin the world over again.[4]

But moving forward will require us to dispense not only with our dreams of apocalypse but to redefine progress. These days, we are torn between our faith in progress and the growing power of the apocalypse. We wonder: Is everything unraveling? Are we evolving? Do we have to unravel to evolve? Will everything be revealed, or will everything just come undone? When we look toward the future, we cannot decide between placing our faith in progress or in catastrophe.

While many of us have fallen into the dualistic trap of apocalyptic thinking, at least one group has sought to find a way out: the New Age movement. While admirably attempting to create an alternative to both religious fundamentalism and economic globalization, however, the New Age movement unfortunately continues to rely on both. Since at least the end of the Cold War, New Age believers have wholeheartedly embraced the notion that the only way forward is by achieving some sort of spiritual globalization—a Great Turning, a Transformation, or a Consciousness Shift. As to exactly how this shift in consciousness will take place, New Agers remain ambivalent. On one hand, many writers have viewed this spiritual transformation in evolutionary and progressive terms, borrowing from Darwin to explain consciousness as a force evolving in complexity and capacity. That any evolutionary biologist such as Stephen Jay Gould will tell you that evolution is dumb[5]—that is, it has no inherent direction and is just as likely to move toward increasing simplicity as increasing complexity—is conveniently ignored by those New Agers who reach for the evolutionary metaphor when imagining the future of human spirituality and consciousness. One day, they maintain, humanity will achieve a higher level of empathetic consciousness that will transform our relationship to the world. On the other hand (perhaps exhibiting impatience with the glacially slow pace of evolution), New Age thinkers have borrowed extensively from the apocalyptic expectation of religious fundamentalists, anticipating a precipitating, cataclysmic event that will either bring about the sudden arrival of the New Age or preclude it from ever happening.

Whether this New Age will be reached through gradual progress or sudden cataclysm is a question that is never fully resolved. "Though we can discern the great turning and take courage from its manifold activity," writes Joanna Macy, "We have no assurance that it will happen in time. We cannot tell which will happen first: the point of no return, when we cannot stop the unraveling of the systems supporting complex life forms, or the moment when the elements of a sustainable society cohere and catch hold."[6] In Macy's words, the New Age vision wanders blindly in the netherworld between progress and apocalypse. Yet exempted by the New Age's apocalyptic anticipation and patient hope for progress is the possibility that both this transformation and this crisis will continue simultaneously for quite some time— that, within our lifetimes, and our children's lifetimes, and our grandchildren's lifetimes, no assurance will ever come that we have averted "the point of no return."

Still, the New Age movement suffers from no shortage of "visionaries" ready to serve as "elders" to the tribe, to "midwife" a new worldview into being by writing "earth charters" and drafting plans for others to implement when the present worldview has finally collapsed. The practical result of such persistently future-oriented thinking was once made apparent to us at a local "Post Carbon" meeting, at which a group of local progressives had gathered to address how our little community in the desert of Utah might organize itself in preparation for the looming energy crisis. Nearly everyone at the meeting wanted to join the transportation subcommittee and to plan for the time twenty years out when oil and cars would be a scarcity; almost no one wanted to get together to insulate the houses of the town's poor the following week. As with so many people who view the problems of the world through the prism of apocalypse, it is the dramatically transformed world of the future—and not the tangible and sometimes mundane world of the present—that holds the New Age movement's attention. Such eagerness to hold companionship with the future provides little guidance in the present.[7] Should we bring about the change or simply await it, the New Agers wonder, echoing the same apocalyptic question that Paul asked some two thousand years ago?

The end of a worldview will require us to entertain ideas that don't fit into the deeply eroded channels of jubilant progress or a damning apocalypse—not simply re-dressing such ideals in quasi-spiritual overtones. New worldviews begin with needs, not ideas. The Hebrews in Babylon didn't set out to create a new worldview or to lay the foundation for Western civilization's quest for meaning in history; they just needed to believe that their God had not abandoned them when they were exiled from Jerusalem. Those who draft Earth Charters and try to push a fully formed worldview before addressing the pressing issues before us are putting the proverbial cart before the horse: the new worldview will emerge through the process of facing the problems at hand, not before.

When and if the alternative is articulated, it won't be articulated in the old dichotomy of left versus right. It won't be articulated in the old dichotomy of environmentalism versus business interests, it won't be articulated as labor versus management, it won't be articulated as prosperity versus poverty, and it won't be articulated as free trade versus protectionism. It won't be a Marxist critique of capitalism or a feminist critique of patriarchy. When the new way of looking at the world emerges, if the true alternative to our worldview comes into fruition, it will reach above and beyond the parameters of our current worldview, which define and limit what we believe is probable and possible. A true alternative doesn't emerge from within the structures of what is or by recasting the ideas of progress versus apocalypse in Berkeleyite or neospiritual language; it smashes those structures to pieces.

THE LAST MYTH

For more than two thousand years, the apocalypse has been at the center of the Western mind's understanding of history, serving both as a foundation for our religious beliefs and as a foil to our secular ideals. Whether or not a person today actively entertains a personal vision of the end is somewhat beside the point, because all of us—regardless of our individual beliefs—are the inheritors of an intellectual and spiritual lineage in which the idea of apocalypse and the idea of a meaningful history are literally inseparable. As modern people, we can no more escape the influence of the apocalypse in shaping our understanding of history than we can escape the influence of Newtonian physics in shaping our understanding of gravity or Einstein's theory of relativity in our understanding of the movement of galaxies.

Yet the idea of apocalypse hasn't always been with us. For more than 100,000 years, the minds of human beings engaged the world with a fundamentally different view of time than the one we hold today. For traditional humanity, time moved in a circle, and at the center of that circle was myth. The world was stable; it was exactly as it was meant to be, as it had always been, and as it would always be; and this stability and sense of order to the world naturally led traditional humanity's curiosity not to the question of how the world would end up but *how it had come to be*. When they sought meaning, traditional people would turn, always and without exception, to stories of creation. We found meaning in the world—not to mention the tools and tricks for survival—by doing those things that the gods and our ancestors had done before us. In time, this emulation of those who had come before became ritual, and with ritual came belief.

It was through this repetition of archetypical action that historic time was abolished. Romanian religious scholar Mircea Eliade called this process the Eternal Return, a process of repetition and ritual in which "everything begins over again at its commencement in every instant. The past is but a prefiguration of the future ... nothing new happens in the world."[8] In the traditional view, seasons changed, nations rose and fell, people lived and died, and everything was constantly reborn; endings were inevitable and constant and unpredictable, but never final or imminent—the exact opposite of the apocalypse that has long been anticipated by the Western mind.

It was this way for nearly all the human story. The writer Denis Dutton once observed that there have been a mere 120 human generations since Plato, compared to the nearly 80,000 human generations who lived before him.[9] Both the scale of the perspective and the demarcation point offered by Dutton are relevant to our understanding of the apocalypse, for it was only around Plato's time that man began to shift his focus of interest toward a new idea of history as the source of meaning in the world. Beginning from time immemorial and lasting nearly until the first millennium before Christ, traditional man ascribed no meaning to history as we understand it; to the extent that he had an idea of history, he found it profane and instead focused his cosmological gaze on the mythic realm of the gods, who lived at the eternal center of creation.

This focus on myth as the source of meaning in the universe did not change with the advent of agriculture or with the beginning of civilizations. Over time, however, the rise of more permanent settlements and civilizations began to leave long-lasting evidence of the past experiences, accomplishments, and failures of humanity's predecessors. The evidence of ruins presented humankind with the problem of explaining what had happened in the human—rather than in the mythical—past. Where had these people gone?

In answering that question, the idea of history was born. Beginning around 700 BCE, during the Axial Age, a new idea of the Declining Ages of Man spread rapidly throughout the known world as humanity encountered—and sought to make sense of—these ruins of previous civilizations. With the introduction of the idea of declining ages, the idea of historical time began to coexist and compete with the cyclical understandings of time with which humanity had lived for more than 100,000 years.

Yet history, humanity soon found out, was a terrifying place to be. It lacked the sacred metaphysical consolations of myth; historic time was meaningless and random. As long as humanity had lived in myth, we found no reason to escape the world; yet almost as soon as the idea of history originated, we sought to escape it. In this desire to escape from history, the seeds of apocalypse were sown.

It was toward the end of the Axial Age that the Israelite priests, drawing on an evolving view of linear time and then on Persian and Greek influences, began to imagine their God not as one of many in a mythical pantheon of gods but as an omnipotent God who played an active role in the political history of the empires that were making and remaking the map of the ancient world. Influenced by Zoroastrianism's solution to the problem of historicity—the Persians recast history as a battle between good and evil, with a measured terminus—the Israelites made a radical departure from previous Mesopotamian beliefs. Instead of being a meaningless, profane place, history for the Israelites became the place where God unveiled his plan for his chosen people. Repeatedly persecuted, enslaved, and slaughtered, the Israelites began searching for revelations of God's plan within the horrific events of their day, longing for the moment when not only would the meaning of history become clear but history itself, with its endless series of trials and disappointments, would come to an end.

With this shift in focus to an escape from historic time, humanity's mythic gaze moved irreversibly from creation to destruction and from the beginnings of the world to its end. People haven't wondered about the end of time since the beginning of time, as is often stated; instead, people have wondered about the end of time since the beginning of the idea of history. This shift in focus toward the end set the stage for the arrival of Jesus Christ, whose mastery of this new apocalyptic anticipation for a radical end to history transformed the world. For the next fifteen hundred years, the apocalyptic understanding that God was in control of history would exert a singular and unrivaled influence on the story of Western civilization.

Yet once history had replaced myth, and God had become Man, it was perhaps inevitable that humanity would seek to replace God as the conductor of history. Beginning less than five hundred years ago among the intellectual elite of Europe, and fueled by the spread of literacy and industry and a new access to previously unimaginable material wealth, humanity began to believe that it could emancipate itself from the enslavement of history's tribulations through the progress of reason, science, education, and industry. History didn't have to decline if humanity could improve.

For a time, this dream of progress competed with the promise of the apocalypse as a source of meaning and purpose to history. History didn't have to end to reveal its meaning; history was what we made of it—and we would make it wondrously better. Yet by the middle of the twentieth century, the great metaphysical story of Western civilization—of the movement of meaning from myth to history, and of the passing of control over that meaning from God to humanity—was at a crisis point. The dream that science, reason, and industry could provide humanity with the means toward achieving a more perfect union on earth began to collapse with the detonation of the first atomic bomb, and the pace of that collapse has only accelerated as the challenges of the twenty-first century—from global warming and peak oil to resource depletion and overpopulation—have revealed themselves to be challenges brought upon us by our own technological and scientific progress.

The great problem that the secular mind now faces is the problem of a declining history without the hope of divine intervention. We are faced with what Mircea Eliade has called the *terror of history*. "In our day," Eliade wrote, "When historical pressure no longer allows any escape, how can man tolerate the catastrophes and horrors of history . . . if beyond them he can glimpse no sign, no transhistorical meaning; if they are only the blind play of economic, social or political forces?"[10] If all of life, of material creation, of nature itself, might now be destroyed by the same progress that once promised to emancipate us from the injustices of history through technological and scientific achievement, then how does the secular mind, with its quasi-religious faith in a better future, provide meaning to and redemption for this thing we call history?

The answer is apparent in the burgeoning apocalyptic anticipation that is all around us. Faced with the evidence that our way of life is unsustainable in a world of declining resources, the secular among us find ourselves turning increasingly not to our faith in human progress but instead to the consolation of apocalyptic thinking.

Since the Enlightenment and the birth of empiricism, science has destroyed the myth of how the world was created and replaced it with an understanding of the big bang, planetary creation, and biological evolution. We've abolished the world of myth and replaced it with history as our source of meaning. We've even come to understand how the world will ultimately end, when our sun goes supernova in five billion years. But the Last Myth that science, empiricism, and rationality has been unable to destroy is the myth of apocalypse—the idea that a moment of clarity will come, when the current world will unravel and the Golden Age will arrive. This Last Myth—this belief that a cataclysmic event will illuminate the meaning of history—is more than a remnant of the Judeo-

Christian apocalypse. It the one mythical archetype that science has been incapable of eradicating from even the most secular of minds—that, indeed, each new discovery of science has only strengthened. Born from our desire that history be meaningful, it has gained strength in every decade since the detonation of the first atomic bomb at Alamogordo. Despite its long origins—origins that reach back more than 2,500 years—and despite the platitudinal insistence that "people have always thought about the end of the world," the increasing potency of the Last Myth—in our widespread expectation of an imminent collapse—is a decisively modern phenomenon.

The purpose of myth, according to anthropologist Claude Lévi-Strauss, is "to provide a logical model capable of overcoming a contradiction."[11] The contradiction the Last Myth seeks to overcome is the contradiction between our Enlightenment belief in progress—in a more hopeful and continuously improving future and in an America that leaves a better world for each succeeding generation—and the growing sense that those beliefs cannot continue indefinitely in a finite world.

It is, of course, much simpler to imagine the Last Myth as merely the obsession of evangelical Christians or cultish freaks and to therefore dismiss apocalyptic thinking as a fringe idea, unworthy of serious empirical examination. It takes a bit more time in the mirror to recognize that the Last Myth is the place where the secular idea of progress has found itself as we enter the second decade of the twenty-first century. And yet here we are. As the dream of infinite progress collides with the limits of the real world, an apocalyptic trance of global proportions is emerging, a trance in which we turn to the Last Myth—the myth that a coming cataclysm, whatever it is, will inevitably reveal our new place in the world.

THE RIGHT MYTH FOR OUR TIME?

Joseph Campbell reminds us that "at moments of psychological danger, [myths] magically conjure forth the life energies of the individual and his group to meet and surpass the dangers."[12] Given the magnitude of the problems we're facing, couldn't the Last Myth be the right myth for our time? Could it be serving the function of spurring us into action, to address the crises we are facing by giving enormous import to these "last days"? Perhaps in this moment of global danger, the Last Myth is exhorting us to change before it is too late. Perhaps through the Last Myth, global warming becomes the moment when we will achieve the dream of a clean, sustainable future; the wars in Iraq, Afghanistan, and Libya become the opportunity to achieve eternal peace and freedom in the Middle East; peak oil becomes the opportunity to return to pastoral living in small communities. Perhaps, one might conclude, the rise of the apocalyptic is a *good* thing, sounding the alarm bells in our cultural consciousness, telling us that we need to address the issues before us or face certain calamity.

After all, apocalyptic rhetoric assures us that our place in history is not just significant but that we are at *the* most significant point in history. This historical narcissism allows us to look back on the Mayans and believe that they were obsessed with our time and to look forward and imagine that future generations will consider our time to have been pivotal in the history of the world. We hear echoes of that same historical narcissism in every election cycle, with politicians declaring that "this is the most important election in history," and that "if we overcome these challenges"— whether they be tackling the deficit or reducing CO_2 in the atmosphere or defeating Islamofascism—then we will arrive in the

Promised Land, and our era will be remembered by grateful future generations as the "defining moment" when "mankind rose above its differences to confront its challenges." Apocalyptic rhetoric provides us with Ernest Becker's "cosmic specialness" and "unshakeable meaning,"[13] for through such rhetoric we become the key players in the climactic act on the stage of history.

Yet more than a dozen years into this era of incessant apocalyptic rhetoric, it is clear that we are butchering our role and are no closer than before to resolving the problems facing us on the global stage. Instead of being impelled into action, we have become divided by the apocalyptic storyline, ignoring the underlying issues that gave rise to the storyline in the first place. The apocalyptic storyline becomes a form of daydreaming escape: the threat of global warming becomes a fantasy to one day live off the grid, or buy a farm, or grow our own food; economic collapse becomes like a prison break from the drudgery of meaningless and increasingly underpaid work in a soul-crushing cubicle; peak oil promises the chance to finally form a community with the neighbors to whom you've never spoken. Yet despite the fantasia peddled by Hollywood and numerous writers, a world battered by natural disasters and global warming, facing declining natural resources and civic unrest, without adequate water or energy or food, with gross inequalities between the rich and the poor, is not a setting for a picaresque adventure, nor is it the ideal place to start living in accord with your dreams.

The deeper we entangle the challenges of the twenty-first century with apocalyptic fantasy, the more likely we are to paralyze ourselves with inaction—or with the wrong course of action. We react to the *idea* of the apocalypse—rather than to the underlying issues activating the apocalyptic storyline to begin with—by either denying its reality ("global warming isn't real") or by despairing at its inevitability ("why bother recycling when the whole world is burning up?"). We sink into arguments as to whether the threats are real or hyperbolic, as we did with Y2K. And as with Y2K, we react to apocalyptic threats by either partying (assuaging our apocalyptic anxiety through increased consumerism, reasoning that if it all may be gone tomorrow, we might as well enjoy it today), praying (in hopes that divine intervention or mere time will allow us to avoid confronting the challenges before us), or preparing (packing "bug-out" packs for a quick escape or stocking up on gold, guns, and canned food, as though the transformative moment we anticipate will be but a brief interlude, a bad winter storm that might trap us indoors for a few days or weeks but that will eventually melt away).

None of these responses avert, nor even mitigate, the very threats that have elicited our apocalyptic anxiety in the first place. Buying an electric car doesn't solve the problem of a culture dependent on endless growth in a finite world; building a bunker to defend against the zombie hordes doesn't solve the growing inequities between the rich and poor; praying for deliverance from the trials of history doesn't change that we must live in the times in which we were born. Indeed, neither partying, nor preparing, nor praying achieves what should be the natural goal when we perceive a threat on the horizon: we should not seek to ignore it, or simply brace for it, but to avert it.

Myth, since time immemorial, has provided humanity with a sense of purpose in daily life. The drudgery of stripping a carcass, or tilling a field, or governing a village was elevated to a new level of significance in the minds of traditional people by its perceived replication of the acts of the gods. Yet the Last Myth provides little direction to our daily actions. Instead, the context of an individual life is always reliant on a future event—an event that never actually occurs, when the final cataclysm will arrive and prove our world-view correct. Rather than a sense of purpose in the thousands of days that we burn through in our lives, we are left with an insatiable longing for what is to come.

BEYOND THE LAST MYTH

Addressing the challenges of a growing global population in a period of declining resource availability—and creating a world-view that comports with, rather than denies or despairs over, the challenges we face in the twenty-first century—will require us to let go of our fears, fantasies, and expectations of apocalypse. Yet moving beyond the apocalypse is no easy task, for it is more than simply a way of thinking about the world and its future. While we may mock or deride apocalyptic thinking when we encounter it in others, it has existed as a constant companion to the Western mind since the rise of Christianity; it has been nurtured, for Americans, by the uniquely religious history of our nation; and it has become widely activated by the horrors of the twentieth century and the looming crises of the twenty-first. The apocalypse is, in other words, not just an idea but an archetype, a metaphysical belief that has taken root at the core of the Western worldview. Archetypes are more than the basis of some mythological stories, more than the means through which we interpret events in the real world. They are, as Edward Edinger once wrote, "devouring mouths—finding little egos they can consume and then living out of those egos."[14] And as Carl Jung said, "One never possesses a metaphys-ical belief but is *possessed by it*."[15]

Put another way: it doesn't matter whether we believe in the archetype of the apocalypse, for the archetype of the apocalypse holds *us*. None of us has escaped its influence.

If our idea of progress is on the verge of collapse, then our apocalyptic anxiety is easily accounted for—for the worldview to which we turn for meaning is growing increasingly meaningless. Yet the further we retreat into that apocalyptic fantasy, the more likely we are to bring about the very apocalypse that we fear. Just as each of us must accept, at some point, our own personal mortality, letting go of the apocalyptic storyline will require us to accept a level of cultural mortality and to let the dream of ruins die. Doing so will result in a rebirth. Mircea Eliade believed that "the anguish of the modern world" was a "sign of an imminent death," but "a death that is necessary and redemptive," for it will be followed by "the possibility of attaining a new mode of being" based on "maturity and responsibility."[16]

The "new mode of being" that we must create is not going to be based on avoidance, or denial or despair, or longing for a future cataclysm to sort us all out and prove our beliefs correct. It's going to be based on coming to terms with the physical world and its restrictions as it is, and recognizing that those realities are fundamentally different—politically, economically, ecologically, and culturally—than the world in which most of us grew up. That world was made magical by an abundance of cheap energy, an energy that fueled a historic rise in material wealth for America and the developed nations; that fueled the dominance of the US dollar as the world's reserve currency; that fueled the rise of the American middle class, the American Dream, and the belief in American exceptionalism; and that fueled, for nearly three centuries, the belief that continued and uninterrupted progress was our birthright.

Yet it also fueled an unprecedented rise in global population—a tripling in the number of human beings in less than a century, with another doubling (from four to eight billion) likely to be completed in the fifty years between 1974 and the middle of the next decade. And as the appetite of developing countries continues to grow in a world already struggling to meet the global demand for resources, and as the ecological effects of climate change and the unwinding of the global credit bubble continue to disrupt the world's economy, the unsustainability of a worldview predicated on cheap energy, cheap credit, and abundant resources is becoming obvious. We may beat our fists into the dirt, or sink our oil and natural gas wells there in hopes of finding energy in such bounteous and efficient levels as we encountered at the beginning of the twentieth century—but it is not there. We may insist that technology will find a way out of this reality or that America deserves to be exceptional by continuing to consume 25 percent of the world's resources despite having only 5 percent of the world's population—but we're not investing in those technologies, and such inequalities rarely last. We may believe that a new global consciousness will emerge to control our insatiable appetites or continue to insist that uninterrupted and unchallenged progress is our birthright—but such beliefs no longer match up with reality, for the dreams and hopes of an emerging global middle class are competing fiercely with our own. This may not be about the decline of America but "the rise of the rest," as journalist Fareed Zakaria put it.[17] Yet the rise of the rest is going to have profound effects not merely on the resources of the world and our way of life but ultimately on the way we view the world.

Within our lifetimes, we're not going to be building a society based on exponential growth, nor are we going to be able to build a "sustainable" society in a world of declining resources. We're going to have to learn to create a society based on decline—a decline in energy consumption, in available resources, and, eventually and inevitably, in human population. This doesn't mean we're going all the way back to the Stone Age, nor does it necessarily presage an apocalyptic collapse; such visions are merely the symptoms of our inability to imagine a world different from our own.

In the century and a half before the Reformation, apocalyptic expectation in the Western world reached a feverish pitch that has rarely been matched in history—except perhaps in our own day. The governing institution of Martin Luther's day—the Catholic Church—was perceived by many as irredeemably corrupt and incapable of addressing the problems confronting society. The indulgences that the Church exacted upon its subjects were seen as increasingly rapacious and arbitrary, draining society of its belief in a just and stable world. The Scholastic method of learning, practiced by monks who tried to resolve the differences between their beliefs and the texts of the ancient world, became an increasingly vainglorious and empty pursuit, producing dizzying works of scholarship without any application in the real world. The world, it seemed, could not continue as it was. Yet nobody could imagine a different world or a new path forward in history: the only way out, so many believed, was through apocalypse.

But the apocalypse didn't happen. Instead, by questioning the very basis of sixteenth-century Europe's worldview—the inerrant authority of the Church—Martin Luther accelerated a process that ultimately overturned not just the Church's stranglehold on Europe but the entire political, intellectual, and spiritual basis for that stranglehold.[18] By questioning the basis of a worldview, a new world was born: the Enlightenment soon followed, and the age of empiricism, science, and rationality gave rise to our own democratic institutions and unlocked the secrets of easy energy and material wealth.

But now that age, too, is coming to an end. That there are limits to growth and progress has been known to us for more than a century. Pick your beginning point: Matthew Arnold's retreating sea of faith, the massacre in the trenches of World War I, the detonation of the first atomic bomb, or the looming catastrophe of global warming. No matter which moment you point to as the beginning of the end, the end of our worldview is already well under way. And as the old worldview deteriorates, our apocalyptic anxiety is rising. This rising anxiety marks a dramatic act in a long intellectual play, to be sure, but the actual resolution—the denouement—lies much further in the future.

Recently, a friend of ours who is in his sixties, observing the great upheaval of the last few years, said to us: "My only regret is that I won't be around thirty years from now to see how it all turns out." This is an understandable desire, felt by many of us when we contemplate the outcome of history as the end of our lives approach. Yet by taking a step back, we recognize the hopelessness of that desire. History ebbs and flows on a scale that dwarfs us. Resolution and permanence are a trick of perception, as when, at the high and low of the tide, it seems as though the sea has stopped moving. Such moments can trick us into believing that the world is in stasis, or that everything depends on our actions on the beach. Yet the sea never stops moving. The rhetoric of the apocalypse gets it backward: this is not the most important time to be alive—being alive is the most important time. The world before us will still be marked by laughter and love and art and joy; a life is no less valuable or beloved if one lives in an age of decline, when the tides are running out, than in an age of progress.

When we free ourselves from the hypnotic spell of apocalypse, when we let go of our desire to see how things will turn out, we are free to answer a more important question. Not, are my beliefs correct? But, how do I live in accord with my values right now? Our insistence that a new world is coming later is a delusion; it is already here. We have met many who say that they will go start an organic farm when things come undone. We have met others who are already farming and say that they are doing it to prepare for the Great Unraveling. Why not choose to farm, as one example, because you value independence, self-sufficiency, and the environment and want to live in accordance with your values, rather than framing your life through the prism of the apocalypse, hoping to be proven right and others proven wrong? The answer as to how to live into our values is different for each of us—it may be about traveling the world as much as manning the ramparts. But the right public policy prescriptions and personal decisions will come only when we abandon our expectations that some future cataclysmic moment will eventually prove us right.

*   *   *

During the twentieth century, a handful of influential thinkers—Joseph Campbell, Mircea Eliade, Carl Jung and his protégé, Edward Edinger—made tremendous advancements in our understanding of the power of myths and archetypes on the human psyche. By the end of their lives, their studies had led them inexorably toward considerations of the apocalypse. The questions they pondered are the questions we now face: given the power of archetypes to manifest themselves in the real world, is the widespread and increasing belief in the apocalypse destined to become a self-fulfilling prophecy? And if the metaphysical journey of humanity can be described as the movement of meaning from myth to history, and from God to man—have we become the gods we once feared?

Carl Jung observed that the development of the atomic bomb gave us the power to unleash the apocalypse on our fellow man. "Not nature, but the 'genius of mankind,' has knotted the hangman's noose with which it can execute itself at any moment," Jung wrote.[19] This same genius of humankind, which unlocked the resources of the earth to build the richest civilization in the history of the world, now threatens to denude and depauperate the earth in its blind fealty and commitment to the ideal of continued growth and material progress. The gods of the traditional world, with their supernatural powers, have been replaced by humans with bombs and shopping lists; the apocalypse has moved onto an entirely secular stage, devoid of divine purpose, sanctity, or meaning.

But having become gods, we must ourselves become more god-like. We must acknowledge that we can no longer wait for the arrival of some other deity—whether Jesus or Mother Nature—to come to resolve our questions in a moment of historical clarity. The future will provide us with no greater insights than the present. Indeed, when the moorings of our world actually come undone, most of us don't acknowledge it: global warming is turned into a belief; economic collapse is viewed as behind us; and cheap oil, we insist, will one day come back. To continue to expect a cataclysmic, crystallizing moment leaves us in a state of paralyzed anticipation—blinding us to the reality that much of what we fear is already here, awaiting our attention.

For more than two thousand years, we've looked to the future for that moment when clarity would descend upon us . . . the wrongs of the world overturned . . . the trials of history adjourned. Consider that no such moment is coming. Consider that the veil has already been lifted, and everything we need to know has been revealed. The world doesn't end, not for a very long time. The future is still ours—but the future is not what it was.

Acknowledgments

We began this book in 2004, while in the depths of our own personal apocalypse. Mel had been diagnosed with myalgic encephalomyelitis at the precise moment that the Howard Dean presidential campaign came crashing down, and we retreated to a little guest cottage on a horse farm near Oak Ridge, North Carolina, to recuperate. There we turned to thoughts of the apocalypse in an attempt to find some solace. In our journey back, we began to wonder why our culture has such propensity for apocalyptic thought, especially in times of crisis—the question at the center of this book. Whatever answers we ultimately found, this one is undeniable: facing the apocalypse is easier when done in community, and we are deeply grateful for the community that supported our work on this book over the last seven years. A number of people who read all or part of the manuscript helped improve the final product. Thanks go to Mark Sundeen, for his years of friendship and generous creative and professional advice; to Brooke Williams, whose insights shared in conversation and in reading the manuscript are in evidence throughout this book; to Christopher Ketcham, with whom we always enjoy shooting guns and shooting the shit, but to whom we are most grateful for excising a word upon which no further mention shall be made; to

Adam Gilles, who gave us perhaps our best critical read ever, of any manuscript; to Rahul Mehta, who sent notes of encouragement on Mariah Carey stationery; to Daniel Suelo—the subject of Mark Sundeen's highly recommended *The Man Who Quit Money* (New York: Riverhead/Penguin, 2012)—who has written about, thought about, and (most importantly) *tried to live* the teachings of Jesus more than anyone we have ever met; and to Kiley Miller, whose enthusiasm after reading just twenty pages of a draft gave *us* the enthusiasm to keep going. Others provided support through conversations on Southern porches or while taking long walks in the woods and canyons and historic districts that we called home during the seven-year process of completing the manuscript. For being critical listeners, devil's advocates, and tireless cheerleaders, thanks go to Anthony Cuda and Katherine Skinner; Franklin Seal; Carol Bradsen; Megan McCarty Colón; Krista Guss; Petra Bartosiewicz; Damian Nash; Sheila Lynn; Christy Williams Dunton; Terry Tempest Williams; Richard Schwartz (whose dinner parties in Castle Valley began the conversation that ultimately gave rise to this book); and Julia Ridley Smith (who suffered through an entire weekend of listening to us bicker about the text, on what was supposed to be a writer's retreat for herself in our home, but who at least saved us from the Trailer of Tears). Thanks also go to Joe Costello, whose understanding of politics and its current decrepitude is unrivaled, but whose ultimate faith in American democracy tempered any cynicism that would have otherwise found its way into this book; to Chandra Om and Victoria Fugit, who knew long before we did that the true core of the book would take longer to reveal than our ambition would imagine; to Sallie Hodges and Helene Rohr, for helping Dr. Hopenfear find a voice on KZMU; to Logan Hansen and Laurel Hagan for last-minute photographic willingness; and to Nick Jones, John Reilly, and Catherine Wessinger, who corresponded with us when we first began our research and who sent us reading suggestions, materials, and words of encouragement when the apocalypse as a subject matter appeared insanely intimidating. Folks ask us all the time how you write a book with your spouse; we were lucky to have the support of Michael and Bunny Gilles on the other end of the phone and Nicole Parentice (who often dropped by the house in the middle of the day just to see the latest episode in our domestic writing life; she thought it would make great reality TV). Deep gratitude goes to Carlton Myatt of Greensboro, North Carolina, whose influence changed the direction of Mel's life and ultimately led to this book. Several places influenced our writing deeply: the Servant Leadership School of Greensboro, North Carolina; The Hood; the Shala; the Horse Farm; Kiley and John's place near Black Ridge; and Castle Valley, Utah. Finally, we are indebted to two women who believed in *The Last Myth* and made it happen: Jill Marsal at Marsal Lyon Literary Agency and Linda Greenspan Regan at Prometheus Books.

NOTES

INTRODUCTION:
THE END OF THE WORLD?

1. Nancy Gibbs et al., "Apocalypse Now," *Time*, July 1, 2002, http://www.time.com/time/covers/1101020701/story.html (accessed May 13, 2006).

2. Left Behind FAQ page, http://www.leftbehind.com/06_help_and_info/faq_general.asp (accessed August 2, 2011).

3. "Bush Discusses War on Terror," CNN.com, http://transcripts.cnn.com/TRANSCRIPTS/0603/20/se.01.html, March 20, 2006 (accessed July 6, 2011). The question of President Bush's belief in the apocalypse was the first question asked by an audience member following the president's speech on the Iraq War delivered at the City Club of Cleveland, Ohio, on March 20, 2006. The speech and subsequent Q & A were carried live by CNN, Fox News, and MSNBC.

4. The success of Jared Diamond's *Collapse: How Societies Choose to Fail or Succeed* (New York: Viking, 2005) throughout the 2000s reinvigorated paperback sales of his earlier *Guns, Germs, and Steel: The Fates of Human Societies* (New York: W. W. Norton, 1997), for which he won the 1998 Pulitzer Prize for General Nonfiction.

5. "Bush Discusses War on Terror."

6. Stephen D. O'Leary, *Arguing the Apocalypse: A Theory of Millennial Rhetoric* (New York: Oxford University Press, 1994), p. 28. In chapter 2, we examine in greater detail the evidence showing that not all cultures have been concerned with eschatology—the study of last things—generally, nor with the end of the world in particular. Disabusing oneself of the notion that "people have always believed in the end of the world" is a crucial first step in examining the apocalypse in a critical manner. The idea that all people at all times have believed in the end of

the world is one of those assumptions that is so nearly universal that it seems self-evident; yet the actual evidence, as we shall see in chapter 2, doesn't support the assumption.

7. Dick Cheney, as quoted by James Howard Kunstler, *The Long Emergency: Surviving the Converging Catastrophes of the Twenty-First Century* (New York: Atlantic Monthly Press, 2005), p. 68. Although widely quoted, the attribution to former vice president Cheney is apocryphal. Some sources point to a non-specified television interview with Cheney in the weeks following the 9/11 attacks, in which he is said to have uttered the line. If so, Cheney was likely echoing (or directly quoting) former President George H. W. Bush, who made the statement on the eve of the United Nations Conference on Environment and Development (UNCED)—more popularly known as the Earth Summit or Rio Summit—held in Rio de Janeiro in 1992.

CHAPTER 1: THE APOCALYPTIC DECADE

1. T. S. Eliot, "The Dry Salvages," in *Four Quartets* (New York: Harcourt, Brace, 1943).

2. Jesus Jones, "Right Here, Right Now," on *Doubt*, recorded 1990, SBK Records, compact disc. In the United States, the song peaked at number 2 on the Billboard Top 100 in July of 1991.

3. Francis Fukuyama, "The End of History?" *National Interest* 16 (Summer 1989): 3–18. The essay remains widely available on the Internet, and in this work is cited from http://www.wesjones.com/eoh.htm (accessed August 1, 2011), unless otherwise noted. Fukuyama expanded his thesis into *The End of History and the Last Man* (New York: Free Press, 1992).

4. Fukuyama, "The End of History?"

5. Ibid.

6. Fukuyama, *The End of History and the Last Man*, p. xii.

7. Bill Clinton, as quoted by David E. Sanger, "Clinton in Vietnam: The Overview; Huge Crowd in Hanoi for Clinton, Who Speaks of 'Shared Suffering,'" *New York Times*, November 18, 2000, http://www.nytimes.com/2000/11/18/world/clinton-vietnam-overview-huge-crowd-hanoi-for-clinton-who-speaks-shared.html (accessed August 1, 2011).

8. Fukuyama, "The End of History?"

9. Ibid.

10. Ibid.

11. As quoted by Paul Waterhouse, "Y2K: Through the Looking Glass," http://www.mindjack.com/feature/y2k.html (accessed September 16, 2006).

12. The overhauling of many computer systems in preparation for Y2K represented a major investment in our nation's electronic infrastructure that has paid off in unexpected dividends. See, for example, comments made in 2002 by Rae Zimmerman, professor of planning and public administration at New York University's Robert F. Wagner Graduate School of Public Service, who argued that the electronic redundancies developed by New York City in anticipation of Y2K helped the city respond to the attacks of September 11, 2001. See http://web.mit .edu/newsoffice/2002/terror.html (accessed August 4, 2011).

13. Nancy Gibbs et al., "Apocalypse Now," *Time*, July 1, 2002, http://www .time.com/time/covers/1101020701/story.html (accessed May 13, 2006).

14. Open Letters, http://www.openletters.net/000703/strandberg000708 .html (accessed May 15, 2006).

15. Rapture Index, http://www.raptureready.com/rap2.html (accessed May 15, 2006).

16. Gibbs, "Apocalypse Now."

17. Hal Lindsey, *The Late Great Planet Earth* (Grand Rapids, MI: Zondervan, 1970). The *New York Times* quote is from the publisher's description.

18. Bill Moyers, in his speech accepting the Global Environment Citizen Award from the Center for Health and the Global Environment at Harvard Medical School, December 4, 2004. The speech was widely circulated online at the time and can be found reprinted under multiple titles on the Internet. See http:// www.alternet.org/environment/20666 (accessed May 20, 2006).

19. Ibid.

20. Ibid.

21. http://joelrosenberg.blogspot.com/2006/10/rolling-stone-ezekiel -option-white.html (accessed December 16, 2006). Note: this URL was inactive at the time of publication.

22. Louis Sahagun, "Plotting the Exit Strategy," *Los Angeles Times*, June 22, 2006, http://www.latimes.com/news/local/la-me-endtimes22jun22,0,5277604 ,full.story (accessed December 16, 2006).

23. Chuck Raasch, "In the Headlines, Glimpses of the Apocalypse," *USA Today*, July 20, 2006, http://www.usatoday.com/news/opinion/columnist/ raasch/2006-07-20-raasch_x.htm (accessed December 16, 2006).

24. Kyra Philips and Paula Zahn, as quoted in "CNN or CBN? Phillips Asks Apocalypse Authors: 'Are We Living in the Last Days?'" MediaMatters for America, http://mediamatters.org/items/200607270001 (accessed December 16, 2006).

25. Ross Gelbspan, *Boiling Point: How Politicians, Big Oil and Coal, Journalists, and Activists Have Fueled the Climate Crisis—and What We Can Do to Avert Disaster* (New York: Basic Books, 2005), p. 20.

26. "Earth Warmest in 400 Years, Panel of Scientists Says," *PBS Newshour*, June 22, 2006, http://www.pbs.org/newshour/updates/environment/jan-june06/climate_06-22.html (accessed August 4, 2011).

27. John Heilprin, "Study: Earth Is Hottest Now in 2,000 Years; Humans Responsible for Much of the Warming," *USA Today*, June 23, 2006, http://www.usatoday.com/weather/climate/2006-06-22-global-warming_x.htm (accessed August 4, 2011).

28. Associated Press, "Scientists: Earth Warmest It's Been in 12,000 Years," Fox News, September 26, 2006, http://www.foxnews.com/story/0,2933,215781,00.html (accessed August 4, 2011).

29. Jeffrey Kluger et al., "Earth at the Tipping Point: Global Warming Heats Up," *Time*, April 3, 2006, http://www.time.com/time/magazine/article/0,9171,1176980-1,00.html (accessed May 15, 2006).

30. The phrase comes from Malcolm Gladwell, *The Tipping Point: How Little Things Can Make a Big Difference* (New York: Back Bay Books, 2002).

31. Edgar Rice Burroughs, *The Return of Tarzan* (Chicago: A. C. McClurg, 1913). Burroughs used the phrase repeatedly throughout the Tarzan series.

32. Smaller packages are a sign of "stealth inflation," in which companies reduce the size of a product while leaving the price the same to recoup rising food costs, under the theory that the consumer is less likely to notice the smaller package than a price increase.

CHAPTER 2: THE PAST IS A FOREIGN COUNTRY

1. Terence McKenna in the foreword to John Major Jenkins, *Maya Cosmogenesis 2012* (Rochester, VT: Bear, 1998), p. xxvii. Emphasis ours.

2. See, for example, Associated Press, "Mayan Elder Tired of 2012 Queries," CBS News, October 12, 2009, http://www.cbsnews.com/stories/2009/10/12/ap/strange/main5378465.shtml (accessed December 12, 2009), in which Apolinario Chile Pixtun, a Guatemalan, argues that "the doomsday theories spring from Western, not Mayan ideas."

3. Frank Waters, *Book of the Hopi* (New York: Viking, 1963).

4. Stephen D. O'Leary, *Arguing the Apocalypse: A Theory of Millennial Rhetoric* (New York: Oxford University Press, 1994), p. 28.

5. The details of what prehistoric humans believed about the world will, by definition, never be known to us. Yet the work of the Romanian religious scholar Mircea Eliade—who spent a lifetime studying the beliefs of ancient prehistoric people, penning nearly two dozen books on the subject—is particularly helpful in understanding the importance of time and myth to the prehistoric mind and illuminating the broad parameters of the prehistoric worldview. (By the middle of the twentieth century, Eliade was arguably the most popular religious scholar in the world; his *Myth of the Eternal Return, or Cosmos and History* [New York: Pantheon Books, 1954] was a commercial success and remains in print to this day. Unlike Joseph Campbell, however, he never did an extended interview with Bill Moyers, and today his work remains largely eclipsed by Campbell's.)

6. Mircea Eliade, *The Myth of the Eternal Return, or Cosmos and History* (Princeton, NJ: Princeton University Press, 1971), p. 5.

7. Ibid., p. 141.

8. Ibid., p. xiii.

9. Ibid., p. 5.

10. Jace Weaver, *Other Words: American Indian Literature, Law, and Culture* (Norman: University of Oklahoma Press, 2001), pp. 260–61.

11. Richard Alleyne, "Amazonian Tribe Has No Calendar and No Concept of Time," *Telegraph*, May 20, 2011, http://www.telegraph.co.uk/science/science-news/8526287/Amazonian-tribe-has-no-calendar-and-no-concept-of-time.html (accessed July 3, 2011).

12. Richard Erdoes and Alfonso Ortiz, *American Indian Myths and Legends* (New York: Pantheon Books, 1985), p. 498.

13. Norman Cohn, *Cosmos, Chaos, and the World to Come: The Ancient Roots of Apocalyptic Faith*, 2nd ed. (New Haven, CT: Yale Nota Bene, 1995), p. 165.

14. See Joseph Campbell, *The Historical Atlas of World Mythology, Vol. 1: The Way of the Animal Powers* (New York: Alfred van der Marck, 1983) and *The His-*

torical Atlas of World Mythology, Vol. II: The Way of the Seeded Earth (New York: Harper & Row, 1989), as well as the summary of the proposed series of books at http://en.wikipedia.org/wiki/Historical_Atlas_of_World_Mythology (accessed July 15, 2011). Campbell died before he could complete all four proposed volumes tracing the evolution of myth from prehistory through the modern era.

15. Cohn, *Cosmos, Chaos, and the World to Come*, pp. 36–37.

16. Ibid., p. 36.

17. Ibid., p. 37.

18. Ibid., p. 9.

19. Ibid., p. 26. Cohn notes that while each Egyptian king was viewed as "the tireless defender of cosmos, ever victorious against the agents of chaos," the Egyptians themselves "did not welcome novelty.... The Egyptian ideal was not so much endless...as [it was] periodic regeneration and rejuvenation, repeated endlessly."

20. L. P. Hartley, *The Go-Between* (London: Hamish Hamilton, 1953), p. 7.

21. Cohn, *Cosmos, Chaos, and the World to Come*, p. 57.

22. The figurine is known today as the Dancing Girl of Mohenjo-Daro.

23. Other names for what we call the Declining Ages of Man include the cosmogenic round, the Ages of Man, the Eternal Return, the Universal Round, or simply the Wheel of Time (or Life).

24. Jerry L. Walls, *The Oxford Handbook of Eschatology* (Oxford: Oxford University Press, 2008), pp. 171–73, and *Wikipedia*, "Yuga," http://en.wikipedia.org/wiki/Yuga (accessed July 3, 2007).

25. *Wikipedia*, "Kali Yuga," http://en.wikipedia.org/wiki/Kali_Yuga (accessed July 3, 2007).

26. Karen Armstrong, *The Battle for God: A History of Fundamentalism* (New York: Random House, 2001), pp. xiv–xv. Also see William Strauss and Neil Howe, *The Fourth Turning: What the Cycles of History Tell Us about America's Next Rendezvous with Destiny* (New York: Broadway Books, 1997), pp. 28–33.

27. *Wikipedia*, "Axial Age," http://en.wikipedia.org/wiki/Axial_age (accessed July 3, 2007). See also Strauss and Howe, *The Fourth Turning*, p. 31, and O'Leary, *Arguing the Apocalypse*, p. 5.

28. *Wikipedia*, "Philosophy of History," http://en.wikipedia.org/wiki/Philosophy_of_history (accessed July 5, 2007).

29. Strauss and Howe, *The Fourth Turning*, p. 29.

30. Joseph Campbell, *The Hero with a Thousand Faces* (Princeton, NJ:

Princeton University Press, 1968), p. 265. See also *Wikipedia*, "Philosophy of History."

31. Eliade, *The Myth of the Eternal Return*, p. 114.

32. Walls, *The Oxford Handbook of Eschatology*, p. 171.

33. Synthia Andrews and Colin Andrews, *The Complete Idiot's Guide to 2012: An Ancient Look at a Critical Time* (New York: Alpha Books, 2008), pp. 62–75.

34. Ibid.

35. John A. Grim, "Apocalyptic Spirituality in the Old and New Worlds: The Revisioning of History and Matter," *Teilhard Studies* 27 (Fall 1992): 8.

36. Andrews and Andrews, *The Complete Idiot's Guide to 2012*, p. 75.

37. *Wikipedia*, "Great Year," http://en.wikipedia.org/wiki/Great_year (accessed April 5, 2011).

38. *Wikipedia*, "Mesoamerican Long Count Calendar," http://en.wikipedia.org/wiki/Mesoamerican_Long_Count_calendar (accessed April 4, 2011).

39. O'Leary, *Arguing the Apocalypse*, p. 48. O'Leary writes: "It is apparent in the various doctrines of world ages (whether cyclical or linear in form) that all societies [beginning in later antiquity] agree in situating humanity at the end of a progressive cosmic decline. No symbol system has yet been discovered that posits a progression from an Edenic golden age to a period of catastrophic evils while locating humanity closer to the point of origin than to the point of ending. The religious imagination never fails to place humankind in the Kali Yuga or the Iron Age; in the mythic awareness of temporality, the present is always the time of greatest evil." While O'Leary's observation is correct, it is a mistake to too tightly conflate later ancient cultures' placement of humanity in a declining age with our own modern vision of apocalypse.

CHAPTER 3: THE EVOLUTION OF THE APOCALYPSE

1. Trade between the Indus valley and Mesopotamia likely dates as far back as 2000 BCE; by the time of Cyrus the Great and the Achaemenid Empire (circa 500 BCE), the link between Greece and India was complete. Evidence shows that trade between Egypt and India was firmly established by the time of Ptolemaic dynasty (305–30 BCE), but it likely began much earlier.

2. Throughout the Old Testament, for example, the Lord frequently refers to himself in the first-person plural ("we"), suggesting later revisions were made to turn the earlier stories of multiple gods in the Israelite tradition into a later story of one God. See Norman Cohn, *Cosmos, Chaos, and the World to Come: The Ancient Roots of Apocalyptic Faith*, 2nd ed. (New Haven, CT: Yale Nota Bene, 1995), pp. 130–36.

3. Exodus 32:1–35. To further the point about the enduring strain of polytheism, one can view the Israelites' Arc of the Covenant, the tent and the tabernacle containing the Ten Commandments that the Israelites carried with them in the years following their Exodus from Egypt, as a sort of temple to their patron-god-among-gods, a mobile version of the ziggurats that the Babylonians were then busily constructing for Marduk.

4. Genesis 17:1–21.

5. Daniel 11:1–12:1. The assertion that it's the longest prophecy in the Bible comes from James Tabor in the wonderful *PBS Frontline* documentary available at http://www.pbs.org/wgbh/pages/frontline/shows/apocalypse/explanation/bdaniel.html (accessed May 6, 2007).

6. Daniel 12. Also see Cohn, *Cosmos, Chaos, and the World to Come*, p. 174.

7. 2 Samuel 7:16.

8. Cohn, *Cosmos, Chaos, and the World to Come*, p. 148.

9. Ibid., p. 143.

10. Ibid., pp. 148–49.

11. Ibid., pp. 152–53.

12. Ibid., p. 157.

13. According to the Old Testament version of events, at least. Other evidence suggests the conquest was entirely bloodless and was made possible in part by a coup by the priests of Marduk.

14. Cohn, *Cosmos, Chaos, and the World to Come*, p. 202.

15. Isaiah 45:4. It is generally believed by scholars that the Book of Isaiah was written by multiple authors over many centuries. Chapters 1–39 are thought to be the work of the original prophet Isaiah, who lived in the eighth century BCE, while chapters 40–55 are believed to have been written by a single author living in Babylon during the exile. Hence, "Second Isaiah." See Cohn, *Cosmos, Chaos, and the World to Come*, p. 151.

16. As had been promised in Isaiah 55:12.

17. Two of those beliefs—a belief in linear time and a dualistic worldview—

were already existent in the Hebraic cosmology, although Persian influence appears to have cemented them in the Judaic religion. The other two beliefs—one in a final, climactic battle marking the end of history, and the other in a final judgment of the dead—most likely did not exist in the Judaic tradition before the Persian occupation of Judea.

18. Frederic J. Baumgartner, *Longing for the End: A History of Millennialism in Western Civilization* (New York: St. Martin's, 1999), p. 10.

19. Ibid., p. 13.

20. The expectation of a messiah during the exile in Babylon had merely been for a military leader who would allow the Jewish people to return to the Promised Land. See also Cohn, *Cosmos, Chaos, and the World to Come*, p. 222.

21. Matthew 24.

22. Baumgartner, *Longing for the End*, p. 19.

23. Matthew 24:35; Mark 13:30; Luke 21:32.

24. Cohn, *Cosmos, Chaos, and the World to Come*, pp. 203–207.

25. Ibid.

26. 1 Corinthians 7:29.

27. It was about this time, not incidentally, that the synoptic Gospels—containing the Olivet discourse and Jesus's vision of the temple's destruction—were written in 70 CE. Thus, whether Jesus ever actually spoke about the destruction of the temple, or whether that remains a late example of apocalyptic conceit in the New Testament remains an open question.

28. Baumgartner, *Longing for the End*, p. 26.

29. Revelation 22:20.

30. John 14:6.

31. John 5:24–25.

32. John 3:18.

33. John 17:11–16.

34. See L. Michael White, as quoted in the discussion about Augustine at "Apocalypticism Explained: The Book of Revelation," Frontline, http://www.pbs .org/wgbh/pages/frontline/shows/apocalypse/explanation/brevelation.html (accessed August 10, 2011).

35. Paul Boyer, *When Time Shall Be No More: Prophecy Belief in Modern American Culture* (Cambridge, MA: Belknap Press of Harvard University Press, 1994), p. 49.

36. Ibid.

37. 1 Timothy 1:3–7.

38. Stephen D. O'Leary, *Arguing the Apocalypse: A Theory of Millennial Rhetoric* (New York: Oxford University Press, 1994), p. 49.

39. Or did, until the more politically correct BCE (before the Common Era) and CE (of the Common Era) replaced the Christian Anno Domini.

40. O'Leary, *Arguing the Apocalypse*, p. 49.

41. Contrary to popular opinion, the virus did not break out into millennial hysteria as the year 1000 CE approached, as the ideas of Bede had not yet trickled down from the Church to the man in the fields, and different people still followed different calendars.

42. Boyer, *When Time Shall Be No More*, p. 52.

43. Baumgartner, *Longing for the End*, pp. 74–80.

44. Ibid., pp. 79–80.

45. Boyer, *When Time Shall Be No More*, p. 61.

46. Martin Luther as quoted by Jerry L. Walls, *The Oxford Handbook of Eschatology* (Oxford: Oxford University Press, 2008), p. 373.

47. Boyer, *When Time Shall Be No More*, p. 58.

48. Walls, *The Oxford Handbook of Eschatology*, p. 374.

CHAPTER 4: THE RAPTURE OF AMERICA

1. Daniel Wojcik, *The End of the World as We Know It: Faith, Fatalism, and Apocalypse in America* (New York: New York University Press, 1997), pp. 24–25.

2. Ibid., p. 26. Peanut butter and graham crackers evolved from the same dietary preoccupation with the end of the world in early nineteenth-century America.

3. John Winthrop, "A Model of Christian Charity," 1630, http://religious freedom.lib.virginia.edu/sacred/charity.html (accessed August 8, 2011).

4. Wojcik, *The End of the World as We Know It*, p. 23.

5. "Public Sees a Future Full of Promise and Peril," PewResearchCenter-Publications, June 22, 2010, http://pewresearch.org/pubs/1635/future-life-2050 -computers-cancer-cure-space-travel-energy-world-war-terrorist-jesus-return (accessed August 8, 2011).

6. The Jewish and Christian tradition of understanding history was progressive only to the extent that God was seen as progressively revealing more of his universal plan and celestial expectations to humanity, from the Burning Bush to the Incarnation.

7. Robert A. Nisbet, *History of the Idea of Progress* (New York: Basic Books, 1980), pp. 21–32.

8. The quote is a slightly bastardized and abbreviated summary of what Galileo actually wrote in *Il Saggiatore*: "Philosophy is written in . . . the universe— . . . but it cannot be understood unless one first learns to understand the language. . . . It is written in the language of mathematics" (as quoted in Peter K. Machamer, *The Cambridge Companion to Galileo* [New York: Cambridge University Press, 1998], p. 65). For a seventeenth-century thinker like Galileo, the study of natural philosophy was, of course, inseparable from the study of God; *Il Saggiatore* was dedicated to the pope (see Machamer, p. 201). Hence, the imprecise (though not necessarily inaccurate) pithy quote that appears in the sig lines of quasi-spiritualistic math nerds the world over.

9. Carl Linnaeus (1707–1778) laid the foundation for the modern system of classifying species using binomial nomenclature, in other words, by genus and species. Although not an evolutionist himself, his system (later much revised) arguably led to the question of not just *how* species were related but how they had come to be so.

10. Friedrich Nietzsche, *The Gay Science*, sect. 125, transl. Walter Kaufmann (New York: Vintage Books, 1974).

11. Paul Boyer, *When Time Shall Be No More: Prophecy Belief in Modern American Culture* (Cambridge, MA: Belknap Press of Harvard University Press, 1994), p. 72.

12. Herman Melville, as quoted by Boyer, *When Time Shall Be No More*, p. 228. The original source is Herman Melville, *White-Jacket; or, The World in a Man-of-War* (New York: Harper and Brothers, 1850).

13. The term was coined by English historian of science William Whewell and eventually replaced the more common term "natural philosophers," which had been used in the centuries since the Renaissance to describe those interested in the workings of the natural world.

14. Wojcik, *The End of the World as We Know It*, p. 34.

15. *Topeka Daily Capital*, August 27, 1881, reproduced at http://www.bread oflifebiblestudy.com/Lessons/20Prophecy&End-Times/Articles/PostTrib07.pdf (accessed August 8, 2011).

16. Boyer, *When Time Shall Be No More*, p. 97.

17. 1 Thessalonians 4:16–17.

18. Darby believed that the promises God had made to Israel would be ful-

filled at the end of time, when the Israelites would be given a chance to accept Christ as their savior before he began his thousand-year reign from Jerusalem. The Bible, Darby claimed, could be read as a series of seven dispensations, or messages, meant for either the nation of Israel or for Christians. The contradictions that seemed to appear in the Bible were caused by confusion over whom each of the messages were meant for: Christians or Jews. See Wojcik, *The End of the World as We Know It*, p. 35, as well as Eugen Weber, *Apocalypses: Prophecies, Cults, and Millennial Beliefs through the Ages* (Cambridge, MA: Harvard University Press, 1999), p. 182.

19. Boyer, *When Time Shall Be No More*, p. 88.

20. Ibid., pp. 90–92.

21. Cyrus Scofield, *The Scofield Reference Bible* (New York: Oxford University Press, 1909), title page.

22. Boyer, *When Time Shall Be No More*, p. 98.

23. Ibid., pp. 95–97. See also Wojcik, *The End of the World as We Know It*, p. 36.

24. The kingdom on earth—the literal thousand-year reign of Christ long anticipated by evangelicals—became a metaphor in the face of a nuclear world; since 1945, eternity has largely been imagined as happening elsewhere. See Boyer, *When Time Shall Be No More*, pp. 115–51.

25. Hal Lindsey, *There's a New World Coming: A Prophetic Odyssey* (Santa Ana, CA: Vision House, 1973), p. 306

26. Wilbur Smith, as quoted in Boyer, *When Time Shall Be No More*, pp. 119–20.

27. Ibid., p. 5.

28. Ibid., p. 137.

29. Pat Robertson, as quoted in Boyer, *When Time Shall Be No More*, p. 138.

30. Boyer, *When Time Shall Be No More*, pp. 140–45.

31. Charles Darwin, *The Origin of Species*, 1859, http://public.wsu.edu/~wldciv/world_civ_reader/world_civ_reader_2/darwin.html (accessed August 8, 2011).

32. See Paul Fussell, *The Great War and Modern Memory* (New York: Oxford University Press, 1975) and also Modris Eksteins, *Rites of Spring: The Great War and the Birth of the Modern Age* (Boston: Mariner/Peter Davison, 2000).

33. Of course, many secular humanists didn't and don't see the extension of rationalism as nihilism.

34. F. Scott Fitzgerald, *The Great Gatsby* (New York: Charles Scribner's Sons, 1925), p. 115. Page numbers vary by edition. Credit for the Gatsby quote as well as Arnold's, Tennyson's, and Hardy's must go to Van Wishard, whose insightful address on the second anniversary of the 9/11 attacks was influential in the writing of this section. See Van Wishard, "Sleepwalking through the Apocalypse," World-TrendsResearch, http://www.worldtrendsresearch.com/articles/presentations/sleepwalking-through-the-apocalypse.php (accessed April 19, 2007).

35. Matthew Arnold, "Dover Beach," in *New Poems* (London: Macmillan, 1867).

36. Alfred Lord Tennyson, "In Memoriam," 1849.

37. Thomas Hardy, "God's Funeral," in *Satires of Circumstance* (London: Macmillan, 1914).

38. Henry David Thoreau, *Walden; or, Life in the Woods* (Boston: Ticknor and Fields, 1854). Page numbers vary by edition.

39. It was only 1979 when Walter Alvarez proposed the theory that is now widely understood as fact: that the most famous mass-extinction event in history, at the end of the Cretaceous period, was caused by the impact of a massive asteroid that crashed into the Yucatán Peninsula some sixty-five million years ago. The impact wiped out the dinosaurs and nearly 85 percent of the rest of life on earth, making way (eventually) for the rise of mammals and that sharp-looking person you see in the mirror each morning.

40. How often do meteors and comets actually impact Earth? At least 185 major craters have been identified, indicating that large impacts between Earth and major meteors are not, geologically speaking, all that rare. Nor are they confined to the distant geological past; as recently as 1908, a large comet entered the Earth's atmosphere in northern Siberia, exploding over the Podkamennaya Tunguska River with a force a thousand times more powerful than the bomb dropped on Hiroshima, knocking down more than eighty million trees over more than eight hundred square miles. Just 12,900 years ago, scientists recently hypothesized, a similar comet streaked across the Pleistocene sky and exploded over Canada, unleashing a shock wave more powerful than millions of nuclear weapons detonating at once, igniting continent-wide wildfires across North America and sounding the death knell not just for the woolly mammoth, the saber-toothed cat, the American camel, and the giant ground sloth (all of which disappeared mysteriously from North America at that time), but also for the Clovis culture, whose prehistoric culture collapsed during the same period. (See Christopher Lee, "New

Theory on Old Debate: Comet Killed the Mammoth," *Washington Post*, June 11, 2007, http://www.washingtonpost.com/wp-dyn/content/article/2007/06/10/AR2007061000915.html [accessed June 12, 2007].) And just 2,800 years before Christ, according to environmental archaeologist Bruce Masse, a three-mile-wide comet crashed into the Indian Ocean off the coast of Madagascar, sending six-hundred-foot-high tsunamis crashing into the world's coastlines and plunging the planet into darkness for nearly a week as superheated water vapor formed massive hurricanes around the globe, killing up to 80 percent of the world's human population. The record of that impact, according to Masse, lies not just in the geologic but also in the mythical record: the aftereffects of the impact, Masse contends, form the basis for the nearly universal story of the Great Flood. (Scott Carney, "Did a Comet Cause the Great Flood?" *Discover Magazine*, November 2007, http://discovermagazine.com/2007/nov/did-a-comet-cause-the-great-flood/article_view?b_start:int=1&-C= [accessed January 5, 2008].) Yet while science, the media, and Hollywood have made images of meteor impacts more available to us, the probability of a major meteor strike wiping out life on earth remains remarkably low. Smaller comets (on a relative scale) such as the Tunguska event or the comet that likely took out the Clovis culture happen perhaps once in ten thousand years; impacts from asteroids, such as the Chicxulub impact that wiped out the dinosaurs, happen perhaps once every hundred million years—and conceivably could never happen again.

CHAPTER 5: THE APOCALYPSE WILL TAKE A LITTLE WHILE

1. Barry Glassner, *The Culture of Fear: Why Americans Are Afraid of the Wrong Things* (New York: Basic Books, 1999), p. xxix.

2. Despite the crowing from some corners that this proliferation of non-mainstream channels will bring Americans more choice and information than they can possibly swallow, the clear effect twenty-four-hour news has had on increasing our anxiety suggests that the our changing and ever-expanding media landscape is likely to produce more fear than freedom.

3. Richard Nixon, as quoted by Glassner, *The Culture of Fear*, p. xxviii.

4. Steven L. Salzberg et al., "Large-Scale Sequencing of Human Influenza Reveals the Dynamic Nature of Viral Genome Evolution," *Nature* 437 (October

2005): 1162–66, http://www.nature.com/nature/journal/v437/n7062/full/nature04239.html#B3 (accessed August 8, 2011).

5. Larry Elliott, "Bird Flu 'Could Be 21st-Century Black Death,'" *Guardian*, January 27, 2006, http://www.guardian.co.uk/business/2006/jan/27/birdflu.health (accessed March 7, 2007).

6. *Wikipedia*, "Black Death," http://en.wikipedia.org/wiki/Black_Death (accessed March 13, 2007).

7. http://webpub.allegheny.edu/group/plague/society.htm (accessed March 13, 2007). Note: this URL was inactive at the time of publication.

8. Ibid. See also Norman F. Cantor, *In the Wake of the Plague: The Black Death and the World It Made* (New York: Harper Perennial, 2002).

9. http://www.sfgate.com/cgibin/article.cgi?f=/c/a/2006/02/19/INGDDH8E2T1.DTL (accessed March 14, 2007). Note: this URL was inactive at the time of publication.

10. Benjamin Friedman, "Think Again: Homeland Security," *Foreign Policy*, July 1, 2005, http://www.foreignpolicy.com/articles/2005/07/01/think_again_homeland_security (accessed March 14, 2007).

11. Patrick Worsnip, "2008 Confirmed Rise in Weather Disasters: Red Cross," Reuters, June 16, 2009, http://uk.reuters.com/article/2009/06/16/us-climate-disasters-idUKTRE55F6K520090616 (accessed August 10, 2011).

12. Spencer R. Weart, *The Discovery of Global Warming* (Cambridge, MA: Harvard University Press, 2008), excerpts available online at http://www.aip.org/history/climate/public.htm (accessed March 14, 2007).

13. James Hansen, as quoted by Sharon Begley, "The Denial Industry," *Newsweek*, August 8, 2007, http://www.newsweek.com/2007/08/13/the-truth-about-denial.html (accessed April 18, 2011).

14. Weart, *The Discovery of Global Warming*.

15. "Wide Partisan Divide over Global Warming," Pew Center for the People and the Press, October 27, 2010, http://pewresearch.org/pubs/1780/poll-global-warming-scientists-energy-policies-offshore-drilling-tea-party (accessed November 15, 2010).

16. Begley, "The Denial Industry."

17. Ibid.

18. The television advertisement was the product of the Competitive Enterprise Institute. See J. J. Sutherland, "They Call It Pollution. We Call It Life," http://www.npr.org/templates/story/story.php?storyId=5425355 (accessed April 19, 2011).

19. Joel Pett, *USA Today*, December 7, 2009, https://www.nytsyn.com/cartoons/cartoons?start_date=1901-01-01&search_id=439980#395853 (accessed August 2, 2011).

20. Patrick Michaels's 1989 op-ed for the *Washington Post*, as quoted by Begley, "The Denial Industry."

21. A. A. Bartlett, "Forgotten Fundamentals of the Energy Crisis," *American Journal of Physics* 46 (September 1978): 880.

22. Richard Heinberg, *The Party's Over: Oil, War and the Fate of Industrial Societies* (Gabriola Island, BC: New Society Publishers, 2003), p. 90.

23. US Energy Information Administration, "Short Term Energy Outlook," August 9, 2011, http://www.eia.gov/steo/#US_Crude_Oil_And_Liquid_Fuels (accessed August 12, 2011). See also *Wikipedia*, "Oil Depletion," http://en.wikipedia.org/wiki/Oil_depletion (accessed August 12, 2011).

24. Bryant Urstadt, "Imagine There's No Oil: Scenes from a Liberal Apocalypse," *Harper's Magazine*, August 2006, http://harpers.org/archive/2006/08/0081156 (accessed December 15, 2010).

25. Many think we'll never run out of oil because it will become too expensive to extract the final remaining reserves.

26. Joe Costello, "The Oil Yoke," http://www.archein21.com/2009/11/ive-put-forth-idea-for-couple-years.html (accessed August 4, 2011).

27. US Energy Information Administration, "Crude Oil Proved Reserves, Reserves Changes, and Production," http://www.eia.gov/dnav/pet/pet_crd_pres_dcu_NUS_a.htm (accessed August 4, 2011).

28. Tim Morgan, "Dangerous Exponentials: A Radical Take on the Future," *Tullett Prebon Strategy Insights*, issue 5, http://www.tlpr.com/documents/strategyinsights/tp0510_tpsi_report_005_lr.pdf (accessed August 9, 2011).

29. Robert Fanney, "As Oil Majors Chime In, the Reality of Peak Oil Lurches Closer," Associated Content, February 4, 2008, http://www.associatedcontent.com/article/575837/as_oil_majors_chime_in_the_reality.html?cat=27 (accessed August 4, 2011).

30. There are some who argue that world oil production will never enter a period of permanent decline. Often relying on outlandish and unscientific theories—for example, that oil is continuously produced through an abiotic process, rather than through the decay and compression of organic matter—their views are roundly dismissed. On the other hand, those who argue that future developments in technology will allow humanity to find more oil and to extract additional amounts from reserves previously thought to be depleted are usually not chal-

lenging the accepted premise of peak oil; they are simply contending its arrival will occur at a much later date—a filibuster of sorts, based on faith in technology rather than contention with the idea of peak oil.

31. Terry Macalister, "US Military Warns Oil Output May Dip Causing Massive Shortages by 2015," *Guardian*, April 11, 2010, http://www.guardian .co.uk/business/2010/apr/11/peak-oil-production-supply (accessed August 4, 2011).

32. Jared Diamond, "What's Your Consumption Factor?" *New York Times*, January 2, 2008, http://www.nytimes.com/2008/01/02/opinion/02diamond .html (accessed August 11, 2011).

33. According to UN figures. See United Nations, Department of Economic and Social Affairs, "World Population Prospects, the 2010 Revision," http:// esa.un.org/unpd/wpp/index.htm (accessed August 10, 2011).

34. John Vidal, "One Quarter of US Grain Crops Fed to Cars, Not People, New Figures Show," *Guardian*, January 22, 2010, http://www.guardian.co.uk/ environment/2010/jan/22/quarter-us-grain-biofuels-food (accessed August 9, 2011).

35. Blake Hounshell, "A Road Tour of the Revolution," *Foreign Policy*, March 1, 2011, http://www.foreignpolicy.com/articles/2011/03/01/a_road_tour_of _the_revolution?page=full (accessed August 9, 2011).

36. "A Run on the Banks: How 'Factory Fishing' Decimated Newfoundland Cod," *E—The Environmental Magazine*, February 28, 2001, http://www .emagazine.com/archive/507 (accessed August 8, 2011). The cod catch peaked in 1968 at 810,000 tons; by 1991, the catch had collapsed to less than 122,000 tons. In 1992, the Canadian government finally closed the fishery, resulting in 30 percent unemployment in some areas of Newfoundland. To date, the cod still have not recovered.

37. Cornelia Dean, "Study Sees 'Global Collapse' of Fish Species," *New York Times*, November 3, 2006, http://www.nytimes.com/2006/11/03/science/ 03fish.html (accessed August 4, 2011).

38. Michael T. Klare, *Resource Wars: The New Landscape of Global Conflict* (New York: Henry Holt, 2001), p. 19.

39. "Humans Will Need Two Earths, Report Claims," MSNBC.com, October 25, 2006, http://www.msnbc.msn.com/id/15398149/ns/world_news -world_environment/t/humans-will-need-two-earths-report-claims/#.TkqBOX NCA0w (accessed August 4, 2011).

40. Virginia Montet, "300 Million U.S. Consumers Make a Vast Ecological

Footprint," Agence France Presse, October 15, 2006, http://www.terradaily.com/reports/300_Million_US_Consumers_Make_A_Vast_Environmental_Footprint_999.html (accessed August 4, 2011).

41. Ibid.

42. Ibid.

43. Ibid. This increasing profligacy has an illogic all its own. Consider, for example, bottled water. Thirty years ago, bottled water barely existed as a product in the United States. Yet during the Apocalyptic Decade, consumption of bottled water in the United States quadrupled; by 2007, Americans were spending sixteen billion dollars a year—more than they spent on iPods® or movie tickets, and at prices up to four times more expensive than gasoline—on a product that was already available for free from the tap. Frequently, in fact, bottled water literally is from the tap: 24 percent of the bottled water sold to Americans is municipal tap water repackaged by corporations. (Thus, in one out of every four transactions, Americans are agreeing to pay private companies a 9,000 percent markup for the drinking water that they've already paid for with their own taxes.) The cost of bottled water isn't measured in dollars alone, of course. To get the one billion bottles of water that Americans drink each week into our parched little hands requires 1.5 million barrels of oil annually—enough to fuel one hundred thousand cars for a year. Once we've slaked our thirst, we throw out some thirty-eight billion (yes, that's a "b") water bottles every year. This, on a planet in which one billion people have no reliable source of drinking water whatsoever. See Charles Fishman, "Message in a Bottle," *Fast Company*, July 1, 2007, http://www.fastcompany.com/magazine/117/features-message-in-a-bottle.html (accessed September 4, 2007).

44. Anup Shah, "Consumption and Consumerism," *Global Issues*, http://www.globalissues.org/issue/235/consumption-and-consumerism (accessed March 26, 2007). Shah is citing figures from the United Nations Development Programme's 1998 Human Development Report.

45. Lester R. Brown, *Plan B 2.0: Rescuing a Planet under Stress and a Civilization in Trouble* (Washington, DC: Earth Policy Institute, 2006). Available online at http://www.earth-policy.org/books/pb2/pb2ch1_ss2 (accessed March 27, 2007).

46. Ibid.

47. Andrew Bacevich, *The New American Militarism: How Americans Are Seduced by War* (Oxford: Oxford University Press, 2005), pp. 4–5, 19, 56.

48. Francis Fukuyama, "The End of History?" http://www.wesjones.com/eoh.htm (accessed 8/1/2011).

49. Bacevich, *The New American Militarism*, p. 19.

50. Madeleine Albright, as quoted by Andrew Bacevich, "The Normalization of War," *Mother Jones*, April 20, 2005, http://motherjones.com/politics/2005/04/normalization-war (accessed April 14, 2007). This growth of military adventurism abroad has been accompanied—and made possible—by a new growth of militarism at home, a trait that has flipped Americans' long-standing suspicion of military involvement on its head. To a large extent, *Merriam-Webster*'s definition of *militarism* as an "exaltation of military virtues and ideals" and "a policy of aggressive military preparedness" has become synonymous with the bipartisan consensus in Washington, DC, and the leitmotif of country music stars from sea to shining sea. In 2003, *Time* magazine enshrined this new American militarism by proclaiming "The American Soldier," whom it called "the face of America, its might and goodwill," as *Time*'s Person of the Year. The American Soldier, of course, used to also be first and foremost the American citizen, who was reluctant to leave home and family for a military venture that wasn't of absolute necessity. But the transition to an all-volunteer military force following America's loss in Vietnam has allowed American politicians—and American citizens—to enjoy war without consequence or responsibility; war is now, thankfully, something someone else does for us. Our natural humanitarian concerns about the effects of military intervention have been assuaged by an aggressive, decades-long PR blitz to rebrand modern warfare as safe, smart, and sanitary—first witnessed in the clever and clean Pentagon briefings during the 1991 Gulf War that touted America's new "smart" weapons. No longer asked to sacrifice for war—indeed, George W. Bush famously asked Americans to continue shopping to show their patriotism following the attacks of 9/11—and with our consciences soothed by the supposed accuracy of smart bombs, it's little wonder that Americans now regularly place more confidence in the military as an institution than they do in the Congress and the presidency that ostensibly controls it. A 2011 Gallup poll, for example, showed 78 percent of Americans possessed a "great deal" or "quite a lot" of confidence in the military, compared to just 35 percent and 12 percent for the presidency and Congress, respectively. See http://www.gallup.com/poll/148163/americans-confident-military-least-congress.aspx (accessed August 10, 2011).

51. Alan Greenspan, *The Age of Turbulence: Adventures in a New World* (New York: Penguin, 2007), p. 463.

52. James Howard Kunstler, "Shocked, Shocked!" *Clusterfuck Nation*, September 17, 2007, http://www.kunstler.com/mags_diary22.html (accessed August 10, 2011).

53. Today, US defense spending accounts for an astonishing 47 percent of the total annual military spending on earth, with the United States spending more money per year on defense than the combined spending of nearly all its allies and potential rivals. Our most heavily armed competitors and friends—the United Kingdom, France, Japan, and China—are each responsible for less than 5 percent of total military spending. Put another way, the United States spends nearly ten times the amount per year on its military than any of its closest allies or largest rivals. Such spending is necessary to maintain the more than 780 US military bases and garrisons that are now strung across the globe and the six global "central commands" that manage military operations on every continent on earth. See Chalmers Johnson, *The Sorrows of Empire: Militarism, Secrecy, and the End of the Republic* (New York: Metropolitan Books, 2004).

54. Frida Berrigan, William D. Hartung, and Leslie Heffel, "U.S. Weapons at War 2005: Promoting Freedom or Fueling Conflict?" World Policy Institute, http://www.worldpolicy.org/projects/arms/reports/wawjune2005.html (accessed August 10, 2011).

55. "Conflicts since the Cold War," USAID, http://www.usaid.gov/fani/ch04/conflicts.htm (accessed August 10, 2011).

CHAPTER 6: IN DEFENSE OF A WORLDVIEW

1. See Clive Ponting, *A New Green History of the World: The Environment and the Collapse of Great Civilizations* (New York: Penguin, 2007), originally published in 1992, as well as Jared Diamond, *Collapse: How Societies Choose to Fail or Succeed* (New York: Viking, 2005) (see note 4 under "Introduction," above).

2. Joseph Tainter quoted by Diamond, *Collapse*, p. 420.

3. Ibid. Tainter's view has grown decidedly more pessimistic since the publication of his landmark *Collapse of Complex Societies* (New York: Cambridge University Press, 1988). He takes issue with Diamond's use of the word *choose* in the subtitle to *Collapse*, arguing that "[s]ocieties don't choose, they are confronted with circumstances." See the Oil Drum, http://www.theoildrum.com/node/8123 (accessed August 17, 2011).

4. Diamond, *Collapse*, pp. 245–47, 427–43. See also our own discussion of

worldview defense and Terror Management Theory, which follows later in the chapter.

5. Ibid., pp. 79–119.

6. Ibid., p. 219.

7. Ibid., p. 246.

8. Ibid., p. 261.

9. Ibid., p. 258.

10. Ibid., pp. 248–76

11. Ibid., p. 247.

12. Arnold Joseph Toynbee, as quoted at *New World Encyclopedia*, http://www.newworldencyclopedia.org/entry/Arnold_J._Toynbee (accessed August 10, 2011).

13. Ernest Becker, *The Denial of Death* (New York: Free Press, 1973), p. xvii.

14. Ibid., p. 5.

15. Ibid. Emphasis ours.

16. Tom Pyszczynski, Sheldon Solomon, and Jeff Greenberg, *In the Wake of 9/11: The Psychology of Terror* (Washington, DC: American Psychological Association, 2002), p. 16.

17. Tom Pyszczynski et al., "On the Unique Psychological Import of the Human Awareness of Mortality: Theme and Variations," *Psychological Inquiry* 17, no. 4 (2006): 328–56.

18. Alice Beck Kehoe, *The Ghost Dance: Ethnohistory and Revitalization* (Long Grove, IL: Waveland Press, 2006), pp. 14–17, 34–42.

19. Leo Apostel, as quoted by D. Aerts et al., "Worldviews, Science and Us, Global Perspectives," January 6, 2005, http://www.vub.ac.be/CLEA/aerts/publications/2005Introduction.pdf (accessed August 8, 2011).

20. Thomas L. Friedman, *The Lexus and the Olive Tree: Understanding Globalization* (New York: Farrar, Straus and Giroux, 1999), p. 9.

21. Christa Case Bryant, "Surging BRIC Middle Classes Are Eclipsing Global Poverty," *Christian Science Monitor*, May 17, 2011, http://www.csmonitor.com/World/2011/0517/Surging-BRIC-middle-classes-are-eclipsing-global-poverty/(page)/3 (accessed July 29, 2011).

22. World Bank Development Indicators 2008, as cited by Anup Shah, "Poverty Facts and Stats," September 20, 2010, http://www.globalissues.org/article/26/poverty-facts-and-stats (accessed July 29, 2011).

CHAPTER 7: BEYOND THE LAST MYTH

1. See note 7 under "Introduction," above.

2. And completely unrecognizable every thousand years. See David W. Anthony, *The Horse, the Wheel, and Language: How Bronze Age Riders from the Eurasian Steppes Shaped the Modern World* (Princeton, NJ: Princeton University Press, 2010), p. 22.

3. Robinson Jeffers, "The Purse-Seine," in *Such Counsels You Gave to Me and Other Poems* (New York: Random House, 1937).

4. Thomas Paine, *Common Sense* (Philadelphia: 1776).

5. Stephen Jay Gould, *Wonderful Life: The Burgess Shale and the Nature of History* (New York: W. W. Norton & Company, 1990), p. 14. To emphasize his point, Gould observes: "Wind back the tape of life to the early days of the Burgess Shale; let it play again from an identical starting point, and the chance becomes vanishingly small that anything like human intelligence would grace the replay."

6. Joanna Macy, *Coming Back to Life: Practices to Reconnect Our Lives, Our World* (Gabriola Island, BC: New Society, 1998), p. 23.

7. Alluding to the Second Epistle of Clement to the Corinthians: "Now this age and the future are two enemies. . . . We cannot therefore be friends of the two, but must bid farewell to the one and hold companionship with the other." Non-canonical, 2 Clement 6:3–5.

8. Mircea Eliade, *The Myth of the Eternal Return, or Cosmos and History* (Princeton, NJ: Princeton University Press, 1971), pp. 89–90.

9. Denis Dutton, *The Art Instinct: Beauty, Pleasure, and Human Evolution* (New York: Bloomsbury Press, 2009), pp. 23–24.

10. Eliade, *The Myth of the Eternal Return*, p. 151.

11. Claude Levi-Strauss, as quoted by Stephen D. O'Leary, *Arguing the Apocalypse: A Theory of Millennial Rhetoric* (New York: Oxford University Press, 1994), p. 34.

12. Joseph Campbell, *The Masks of God: Primitive Mythology* (New York: Arkana, 1991), p. 370.

13. Ernest Becker, *The Denial of Death* (New York: Free Press, 1973), p. 5.

14. Edward Edinger, *Archetypes of the Apocalypse: Divine Vengeance, Terrorism, and the End of the World* (Chicago: Open Court, 2002), p. 5.

15. Carl Jung, as quoted in *The Portable Jung*, ed. Joseph Campbell (New York: Viking Penguin, 1971), p. 628.

16. Mircea Eliade, *Myths, Dreams and Mysteries: The Encounter between Contemporary Faiths and Archaic Realities* (New York: Harper & Row, 1967), p. 237.

17. Fareed Zakaria, *The Post-American World* (New York: W. W. Norton, 2008), p. 1.

18. This process of questioning the basis of the worldview began 150 years earlier, at the dawn of the Renaissance.

19. Carl Jung quoted in Campbell, *The Portable Jung*, p. 628.

INDEX